THE LIFE OF JESUS
FOR TODAY

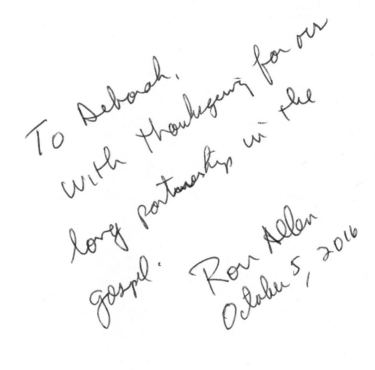

To Deborah,
with thanksgiving for our
long partnership in the
gospel.

Ron Allen
October 5, 2016

Also Available in the For Today Series:

The Apostles' Creed for Today by Justo L. González
The Beatitudes for Today by James C. Howell
Christian Prayer for Today by Martha L. Moore-Keish
Hymns for Today by Brian Wren
The Life of Paul for Today by Lyle D. Vander Broek
The Lord's Prayer for Today by William J. Carl III
Old Testament Prophets for Today by Carolyn J. Sharp
The Parables for Today by Alyce M. McKenzie
The Psalms for Today by Beth LaNeel Tanner
The Ten Commandments for Today by Walter J. Harrelson

THE LIFE OF JESUS
FOR TODAY

Ronald J. Allen

WJK WESTMINSTER
JOHN KNOX PRESS
LOUISVILLE · KENTUCKY

Book design by Sharon Adams
Cover design by Eric Walljasper, Minneapolis, MN

First edition
Published by Westminster John Knox Press
Louisville, Kentucky

This book is printed on acid-free paper that meets the American National Standards Institute Z39.48 standard. ♾

PRINTED IN THE UNITED STATES OF AMERICA

11 12 13 14 15 16 17 — 10 9 8 7 6 5 4 3 2

Library of Congress Cataloging-in-Publication Data

Allen, Ronald J. (Ronald James).
  The life of Jesus for today / Ronald J. Allen.
      p. cm. — (For today series)
  Includes bibliographical references.
  ISBN 978-0-664-23188-0 (alk. paper)
  1. Jesus Christ—Biography. I. Title.
  BT301.3.A45 2008
  232.9'01—dc22   2007031894
  [B]

Contents

Series Introduction   vii

Preface   ix

1. Why a Book on the Life of Jesus?   1

2. The World at the Time of Jesus   10

3. The Realm of God: Focus of the Ministry
   of Jesus   19

4. The Birth of Jesus and the Beginning
   of His Ministry   28

5. Jesus, Judaism, and Conflict with Others   37

6. Realm Themes at the Center of the Teaching
   of Jesus   46

7. Jesus Demonstrates the Realm through Miracles   56

8. Rejecting the Realm: Crucifixion   64

9. The Resurrection: Definitive Sign of the Realm   74

10. Jesus in the Gospel of John   82

11. Jesus in Gospels outside the Bible   91

12. The Life of Jesus for Today   100

Notes   109

Further Reading   115

To
Neill Q. Hamilton (in memoriam)
Darrell J. Doughty
Lala Kalyan Kumar Dey

My teachers at the Graduate School
of Drew University
who encouraged us to think
outside the popular interpretive boxes

Series Introduction

*T*he For Today series is intended to provide reliable and accessible resources for the study of important biblical texts, theological documents, and Christian practices. The series is written by experts who are committed to making the results of their studies available to those with no particular biblical or theological training. The goal is to provide an engaging means to study texts and practices that are familiar to laity in churches. The authors are committed to the importance of their topics and to communicating the significance of their understandings to a wide audience. The emphasis is not only on what these subjects have meant in the past, but also on their present—"For Today."

Our hope is that the books in this series will find eager readers in churches, particularly in the context of education classes. The authors are educators and pastors who wish to engage church laity in the issues raised by their topics. They seek to provide guidance for learning, for nurture, and for growth in Christian experience.

To enhance the educational usefulness of these volumes, Questions for Discussion are included at the end of each chapter.

We hope the books in this series will be important resources to enhance Christian faith and life.

The Publisher

Preface

*W*hen I accepted the assignment to write *The Life of Jesus for Today*, I had two simultaneous but different responses. On the one hand, I felt a flush of excitement at the opportunity to think with readers about the significance of Jesus today. Immediately my mind went to a Sunday in 1959 when I was ten years old. At the end of the sermon in First Christian Church (Disciples of Christ), Poplar Bluff, Missouri, Brother McKim, our minister, offered the invitation to make a confession of faith (to be followed by immersion). As the congregation began to sing, I slipped out of the pew and down the aisle, my heart racing. Brother McKim said he was about to ask me the most important question in life. My answer, he said, would determine the quality of the rest of my life on this earth as well as my eternal destiny. With warmth and love, he took my hand and looked me in the eye and asked, "Do you believe that Jesus is the Christ, the Son of the living God?" When I said yes, a great sense of fullness rose up within.

On the other hand, when I agreed to write this book, my stomach immediately went tight. I thought of an aching irony. Nearly everyone in the Christian community wants to have Jesus on their side of particular issues, but the church is conflicted over how to understand Jesus today. The conflicts sometimes become rancorous. Because of such differences, some Christians are scandalized, some are angry, and some think that others are heretics. It is a strange phenomenon to hold a Bible that calls for us to "love one another" while being attacked by someone holding another copy of the same Bible.

The Life of Jesus Can Be Interpreted Many Ways

The problem, of course, is that the Jesus story can be told many different ways. In this short book, I offer an interpretation of the life of Jesus that includes both how we might locate his life in antiquity and how we might think about his significance today. Seeing the title *The Life of Jesus for Today,* readers may expect the book to be filled with bold statements about what Jesus said and did. However, when writing about the life of Jesus, we deal less with certainty and more with likelihood and probability. I frequently use expressions such as *"likely* happened," *"may* have said," and "biblical scholars *think."* Such language acknowledges the tentative conclusions that we can draw using our sources and methods.

As I said, nearly all Christians I know want to have Jesus on their side, especially with respect to what they want to believe and do. Some readers will be frustrated by the fact that Jesus as I describe him is different from Jesus as they would like him to be. Indeed, I myself wish I could describe Jesus in a way that makes him a mirror of my twenty-first–century values. However, to honor the integrity of Jesus as I think he was in history, I must report what I think was most likely characteristic of him in his own time. The church then needs to explore ways in which Jesus is authoritative for today.

For my part, I promise to be honest about what I think (and not to pussyfoot around), while treating other viewpoints with respect. For the reader's part, I hope this book is a valuable step in a lifetime of discovery and deepening. Even if you cannot subscribe to the picture of Jesus sketched here, I hope that considering it is a valuable experience that helps you come to your own perception of this One.

A Brief Outline of the Book

Chapter 1 sets the stage by considering why a book on the life of Jesus is needed. Chapter 2 describes the world in which Jesus lived. Chapter 3 sets out the main theme of Jesus' ministry according to Mark, Matthew, and Luke—the final and complete manifestation of the realm of God. Chapters 4–9 identify leading motifs in the life of Jesus as witness to the realm, including his birth, his thoroughgoing Jewishness, as well as his teaching, miracles, confrontations with others, trial, death, and resurrection. Chapter 10 focuses on the distinctive perspective on Jesus in the Gospel of John. Chapter 11 turns to stories of the life of Jesus that date from ancient times but are not found in the Bible. The final chapter is a meditation on the significance of Jesus for today.

I hope that the spirit of this book will encourage people to consider how better to love one another. And I pray that this interpretation of Jesus will encourage some readers to embrace God's unconditional love for them and for all, and to resolve to live no longer for ourselves but for God, who loves each and every person (and elements of nature) with unconditional love and who wills for all to live together in love.

1

Why a Book on the Life of Jesus?

Since we have four Gospels that appear to narrate the life of Jesus (Mark, Matthew, Luke, and John), the reader may wonder, Why does the church need yet another book to tell the story of Jesus? There are two responses to this question.

On the one hand, in some circles it is enough to say that the four Gospels together tell parts of one unified story, albeit for different audiences. Many people in this camp say that the Gospel writers wrote documents for widespread circulation. Matthew wrote for Jewish people, Mark for Gentiles (perhaps Romans), while Luke depicted Jesus as savior of both Jewish and Gentile peoples, and John penned a spiritual Gospel that sets out the divine nature of Jesus. From this point of view, a book today might bring the elements of the four Gospel stories into one continuous narrative. This process is called harmonization, as the contemporary reader seeks to harmonize the different notes sounded by the different Gospels. Many church libraries and even some households have a book called a harmony of the Gospels that prints the texts of the four Gospels in parallel columns, and tries to show how they fit together as one story.

On the other hand, another perspective informs *The Life of Jesus for Today*. This idea is that the Gospel writers did not intend to write books for general circulation; instead, the author of each Gospel took preexisting traditions, and shaped them to address specific situations in specific congregations in antiquity. We find an analogy in the situation of today's preacher. Contemporary preachers prepare sermons to speak to the particular congregations they serve.

Matthew, for instance, did not write to Jewish people generally, but sought to address a specific congregation. Nevertheless, I join many other scholars in thinking that we can identify a basic outline of the life of Jesus.

This book follows the second perspective. In this chapter, after considering some basic dates and issues that frame this approach, we note that stories that appear to be from the life of Jesus are often told through the lens of the resurrection. We note how the Gospel writers creatively combined and edited such preexisting materials to form the Gospels as we have them. We end with a short consideration of how to respond to the fact that many of us come to this study with ideas of Jesus already in mind.

Important Dates

Most scholars think that Jesus was actually born about 4 BCE and that he was crucified and resurrected about thirty years later.* His active ministry could have been as short as a few months or as long as three years. To the surprise of many people today, the lifespan of a person in antiquity who reached adulthood averaged only thirty to forty-five years. Thus, Jesus died as a mature adult at the height of his powers.

We do not know the names of the actual individuals or communities who wrote the four Gospels. The earliest written evidence for the use of the names Mark, Matthew, Luke, and John is early second century CE. However, scholars in the tradition in which I move tend to date them as follows:

- The Gospel of Mark was probably written about 70 CE, around the time the Romans destroyed the temple (and much of Jerusalem).
- The Gospels of Matthew and Luke were likely written about 80 to 90 CE, after the fall of the temple.
- The Gospel of John, sometimes called the Fourth Gospel, was probably written after 90 CE.

Because of the order of these dates, when I refer to all four Gospels I refer to Mark, Matthew, Luke, and John.

---

* The expression BCE means Before the Common Era, that is, before the birth of Jesus; CE refers to the period after the birth of Jesus, the Common Era to both Judaism and Christianity.

As far as we know, no one wrote about Jesus during his lifetime. Many scholars think that bits and pieces of the story of Jesus began to circulate in the early communities of Jesus' followers soon after the resurrection, but the first certain written document of Jesus' life, the Gospel of Mark, dates from about 70 CE. What happened to stories of Jesus between his death and resurrection and the writing of Mark?

The Earliest Stories Are about the Resurrected Jesus

We live in a culture that is accustomed to historians and journalists writing factual biographies of famous or important people. Many people today have little interest in serious biography yet still want to know what goes on in the lives of celebrities. We want to know what happened in a factual sense. We would like to have an objective picture of what Jesus said and did as he walked and talked in Galilee and Jerusalem.

However, people in antiquity were not as oriented toward reporting simple facts as we are. Many of their public forms of communication were designed to persuade their listeners or readers to follow the suggestion in the communication. The followers of Jesus who began to tell stories about Jesus after the resurrection told those stories from the perspective of the resurrection. They did not simply report facts about Jesus' life but shaped their accounts in the confidence that Jesus was still alive and active in their midst.

Indeed, in the past thirty years, a number of scholars have discovered that many early communities of Jesus' followers believed that the risen Jesus continued to teach the congregation by speaking to the church through prophets in the community. These prophets received messages from Jesus and spoke them aloud in worship. The Gospel writers wove some of these messages into the stories of Jesus in the Gospels.

Bits and Pieces of the Story of Jesus
Circulated before the Gospels

The followers of Jesus in the early Christian communities told bits and pieces of the stories of Jesus' life. The communities used these materials in their preaching, in educational settings, in worship, and in storytelling. These bits and pieces included elements of his teaching, such as parables and pithy sayings. They also included things that the community remembered Jesus doing, such as miracles, and memories of encounters that Jesus had with other people. The preachers, teachers, worship leaders, and storytellers who used these materials shaped them so that the stories not only recounted the life of Jesus but communicated that the living presence of Jesus was still active in the community.

A miracle story, for instance, did not simply recount a past event. The story expressed the confidence that the figure of Jesus was still present in the community as depicted in the story. A statement of Jesus' teaching was not simply a report of something that Jesus once said but was a living word, spoken afresh by a living Lord.

At some point, the followers of Jesus began to collect materials, perhaps in response to questions within the community and to issues that arose in the community's relationship with people outside. Biblical scholars surmise that there were two early collections of material. One of these collections included stories about Jesus' death and resurrection. Storytellers likely assembled this material to respond to questions about why Jesus was executed and why communities that had gathered around a prophet, now executed, continued to meet and to believe that he was alive. The other collection is known to scholars as Q (from the German word *Quelle*, which means "source"). Although we do not possess a written document containing Q, a reader could identify the contents of Q by going to a synopsis and looking at the points where Matthew and Luke have similar material, but Mark has none. The similar material was Q, and it consists largely of sayings that prepare people for the apocalyptic end of this world, the return of Jesus, and the beginning of a new world (on that motif, see chap. 3). The material in Q appears to be a manual of how to prepare for the apocalypse. Here is an example of material in Q.

Matthew 5:46–47	Luke 6:32–33
(46) For if you love those who love you, what reward do you have? Do not even the tax collectors do the same?	(32) If you love those who love you, what credit is that to you? For even sinners love those who love them.

(47) And if you greet only your brothers and sisters, what more are you doing than others? Do not even the Gentiles do the same?

(33) If you do good to those who do good to you, what credit is that to you? For even sinners do the same.

The wording in these versions differs slightly because Matthew and Luke cast the material to reflect their different concerns.

Four Gospels: Four Stories

The Gospel writers did not know they were writing what would later become part of the Bible. They did not even think they were writing the story of Jesus for posterity. I have already indicated that the Gospel writers were less like reporters for print or electronic media who attempt to report the facts than like preachers or editorial writers who encourage audiences to accept their messages as authoritative interpretations to guide their lives. To use a colloquial expression, we might say that each Gospel writer gave the story of Jesus a particular spin in order to address questions that were prominent in the lives of the congregations to which the writer addressed the story.

The Gospel writers received the bits and pieces of stories about Jesus, but shaped the material to speak to the particular issues in their contexts. Indeed, each Gospel writer rewrote most of the material. The Gospel writers did not simply collect stories of Jesus in the way that a high school student sometimes compiles a research paper by gathering notes on three-by-five-inch cards and arranging them in a pile by the computer and typing the information. The Gospel writers were creative thinkers who used the narrative form to express particular theological interpretations of Jesus and the mission of the church.

From this perspective, each Gospel is not simply a different telling of the story—the same story in different words. From this perspective, each Gospel is a different story.

While Mark, Matthew, and Luke each give the story a particular spin, they share the common perspective of apocalypticism (explained in chaps. 2 and 3). We refer to the first three Gospels as the Synoptic Gospels because the word *synoptic* comes from two Greek words that mean "to see together." John, however, interpreted the story of Jesus

from a perspective that was influenced by a strand of Greek philoso-
phy (explained in chap. 10). While the Gospel of John is sometimes
included in a synopsis, simply flipping through the pages of the synopsis reveals that the chronology and the kinds of material in John are
very different from that found in Mark, Matthew, and Luke, as I explain
further in chapter 10.

Some readers have probably heard of the Jesus Seminar and other
efforts to go behind the Gospels to the historical Jesus, that is, Jesus
as he was as a human figure in the ancient world. The Jesus Seminar
seeks a picture of Jesus that is not interpreted by the Gospel writers
or others. I have no doubt that the Gospels contain some reminis-
cences that go all the way back to the actual figure of Jesus. However,
after a lifetime of study, I conclude we have neither the sources nor
the methods to recover a trustworthy picture of the *detailed* life and
sayings of Jesus. The Gospels are so heavily interpreted that we can
no longer confidently separate the words and deeds of Jesus from how
Gospel writers describe them. Even if we could make such a separation, we would not have enough material to write a complete life of
Jesus or even identify the full body of his teaching.

Common Patterns of the Life of Jesus in the Gospels

While we cannot set out a thorough account of Jesus, Luke Timothy
Johnson, a well-known biblical scholar at Emory University, points
out that we are probably close to Jesus as a figure from history when
we encounter patterns of thought or behavior that are consistent from
Gospel to Gospel.

> The method used to establish this historical framework is one of
> locating converging lines of evidence. It is a simple method,
> based on the assumption that when witnesses disagree across a
> wide range of issues, their agreement on something tends to
> increase the probability of its having happened. . . . Likewise, in
> the case of Jesus, the convergence of one or two points by wit-
> nesses who disagree on everything else is all the more valuable.[1]

Convergence, of course, does not automatically prove historical accu-
racy. But common patterns do suggest likelihood when those patterns

are at home in first-century culture. When sketching an interpretation of the life of Jesus in chapters 3–10, I follow this approach. We cannot achieve a detailed portrait of Jesus, but we can locate main aspects of his ministry in their first-century context.

Reflecting on the Images of Jesus We Bring to This Book

This tentativeness in reconstructing the life of Jesus may make some readers uneasy. After all, many Christians want a picture of a Jesus who is similar to us. We like to have Jesus on our side regarding what we want to believe and do, especially when conflict is involved. Christians like to appeal to Jesus as an authority for their positions on a wide range of life issues—for example, when determining a faithful position on issues such as the death penalty, abortion, same-gender relationships, and war.

The reason for bringing up such matters now is to encourage you to identify and reflect on your perceptions of Jesus as you begin this study. Often we think of Jesus in our own images. To be candid, I would like for Jesus to approve of what I like, and so I tend to imagine Jesus as a version of me—only better. Even when we do not consciously remake Jesus into an image of ourselves, we often read our preexisting perceptions of Jesus into the Gospels and into the church's wider discussions of Jesus.

Some of our views of Jesus result from absorbing the church's historic affirmations of faith, or from conscientious study in Bible school, college, seminars, Bible study groups, or reading. Some of our ideas about Jesus may be so ingrained that we take them for granted and seldom think about them. For example, many of us bring attitudes about Jesus that we absorbed as children in Bible school or confirmation class. We sometimes bring with us attitudes about Jesus that are associated with our gender, ethnicity, social class, or political affiliation.

For example, as a Eurocentric male who is middle class and a liberal Democrat, I would like to find a Jesus whose social views are similar to those of liberal Democrats. I would like to follow a Jesus who allows me to continue my comfortable middle-class lifestyle, and who supports benign male Eurocentric privilege. Some other Christians would like for Jesus to be a first-century spokesperson for family values and other social policies favored by conservative elements in the Republican Party. I am initially uncomfortable when I encounter a picture of Jesus who challenges me. But over time, and through many painful confrontations with discomforting pictures of Jesus, I have learned that such discomfort can be a first step in growth.

I hope readers will bring their preexisting interpretations of Jesus into dialogue with the perspectives in this book. Some of the pictures of Jesus that I have encountered in Bible study groups in congregations and among students and clergy are:

- Friend who walks and talks with us along life's way
- God incarnate, as second person of the Trinity
- One who made substitutionary atonement for our sin
- Risen and ascended Christ, who will return again at an apocalypse
- Representative of middle-class suburban family patterns
- Barrier breaker, who creates inclusive community
- Prophetic challenger of the system
- Liberator from social, political, and economic oppression
- Black Messiah
- The first feminist
- Resister of the Roman Empire
- Living presence

What images of Jesus have you heard that you would add to this brief list?

Given the fact that all human perception is relative, no one has cornered the market on understanding the significance of Jesus for today. I have often found that considering what others think—even if I finally disagree—can help me clarify my own convictions. Perhaps that will be true for you as you make your way through the rest of *The Life of Jesus for Today*.

Questions for Discussion

1. Think for a moment about the associations with Jesus you bring with you to this study. What are they? Where do they origi-

nate—from your past? From issues associated with your gender, ethnicity, social class, or political affiliation? How have these ideas and images changed over the years? How do you see Jesus today? Are you willing to bring this perception into dialogue with other perceptions of Jesus?

2. What does your church teach about Jesus? Who is he? What is his primary work? How do these beliefs compare and contrast with your own?

3. As this study begins, what are some questions that you have about Jesus?

4. Here is an exercise for individuals, classes, or Bible study groups. Go to the church library, the public library, or to your minister and borrow a copy of a synopsis of the Gospels. (Two synopses by Kurt Aland and Burton Throckmorton are listed at the back of this book in "Further Reading.") Have a look at the preaching of John the Baptist in the parallel columns of Matthew 3:1–12, Mark 1:1–8, and Luke 3:1–14. Make a list of the differences and similarities you can find. Which part of the material comes from Q (see above, "Bits and Pieces of the Story of Jesus Circulated before the Gospels")? Which parts are found in only one Gospel? What does each Gospel writer highlight? What do you see as the advantages of working with a synopsis each time you read from a Gospel?

5. How do you react to the idea that we do not have a lot of hard information about the life of Jesus, but have interpretations from the perspective of the resurrection?

The World at the Time of Jesus

When researching the significance of persons from the past, our first responsibility is to get a sense of the persons in their historical contexts. Today's interpreter needs to know what residents of antiquity would have taken for granted about the world of Jesus. When people today have a sense of how it felt to live at a particular moment in the past, we are better able to understand associations and echoes in ancient documents. We can better empathize with the historical circumstances to which those documents were addressed.

When reading about Jesus (and when reading the Bible more generally), people today often project our own questions, fears, hopes, values, and assumptions into antiquity. The technical name for this interpretive move is anachronism—interpreting past situations as if they are little more than reflections of present-day concerns. As much as possible, we want to honor how people thought, felt, and acted in the ancient world.

The aims of the present chapter are twofold. For one, the chapter should provide basic information about the worlds in which Jesus lived—the larger Greek and Roman spheres and his more immediate setting in Galilee and Judea. Second, I hope the chapter helps you begin to imagine how it felt to live in that world.

Alexander the Great's Influence on the World of Jesus

The single most important figure in determining the world of Jesus was Alexander the Great (356–323 BCE). Alexander (who died just a month short of his thirty-third birthday) was a brilliant military commander who conquered most of the nations around the Mediterranean basin. Alexander instituted a policy called hellenization: implanting Greek culture in the lands that Alexander conquered. The designation *hellenization* comes from the Greek word *hellas*, "Greek." Alexander had been a student of the Greek philosopher Aristotle and believed that Greek culture was the apex of human possibility. Alexander, also being shrewd, recognized that a common culture throughout the lands that he conquered would simplify government and commerce.

A centerpiece of hellenization was spreading the Greek language throughout the ancient world. While traditional languages remained in use in traditional communities, Greek eventually became the *lingua franca* of Alexander's empire. Indeed, the earliest manuscripts of the Second Testament are in Greek. Alexander promoted mixed marriages between his Greek soldiers and local women. Alexander established new colonies of Greek inhabitants with Greek religion and culture in the conquered lands, For example, Alexander established the Decapolis, a region containing ten cities east of the Sea of Galilee, mentioned in Mark 5:1–20. Alexander also imported Greek institutions (such as gymnasiums, or schools) into existing cities. Locals could keep their own cultures and religions, but hellenization continuously pressured them to adapt aspects of their lives to the values and practices of hellenization.

After Alexander's death, the forces of hellenization continued. When the empire founded by Alexander ended a few years later, various other nations ruled the land of Israel, but hellenization itself pressed forward. Except for a relatively brief period of independence following the Maccabean revolt (165 BCE to 63 BCE), the land of Israel was under the control of outside rulers during the period that was formative for Jesus, his followers, and followers of other forms of Judaism.

Roman Occupation

In the year 63 BCE, the Romans conquered Jerusalem. For the residents of Judea, the coming of Rome did not mean the end of hellenization but meant its adaptation through Roman expectations. In a savvy move, the Romans did not rule Judea directly, but relied upon local leaders to supervise day-to-day affairs, especially collecting taxes and maintaining order. Herod the Great (who ruled just before Jesus was born) was such an official. At times the high priest functioned as, in effect, a local governor.

During the Roman period, the social system was fairly stratified, with a few people of privilege at the top to whom others deferred. In public social settings, people were treated according to their social status. People from lower social circles had to seek the patronage of people above them. In essence, people in the lower strata became clients of those in the upper strata, who were themselves clients of the Roman emperor.

Much of the land was in the hands of a small aristocratic group; absentee ownership was common. Economic conditions were unstable, and significant numbers of people were in poverty, with some becoming indentured servants either to pay debts or to accumulate resources that would contribute to their later economic advantage. Indeed, for some folk, indentured servitude was a means for social advancement.

The Romans allowed indigenous groups to maintain their own cultures, including the practice of traditional religions (such as Judaism). However, the Roman political and military system required vast amounts of cash, so taxation was heavy. The Romans built their now-famous system of roads to connect the various parts of the empire in order to facilitate the movement of goods and soldiers.

Scholars are divided, however, on the degree to which the Roman occupation had the qualities of a Nazi-like reign of terror or was firm but relatively permissive (except for repressing threats to civil stability).[1] The point at which most scholars think that Rome exercised a heavy hand was in quelling civil disturbance. The Romans typically responded to such threats by immediately putting the perpetrators to death. After a revolt in 4 BCE, the Romans crucified about two thousand rebels.

The Romans had no direct presence in Galilee but relied on local officials to maintain order. In Jerusalem, the Romans relied upon local residents to maintain the peace but also housed a Roman governor there with a small military garrison. The Romans increased the size of the military force during major religious festivals when large crowds came to Jerusalem and the possibility for riot increased. To Christians today, the best-known Roman prefect was Pontius Pilate, who was stern and brutal. The Roman government alone had the power to put people to death. The death penalty was typically meted out for sedition.

Of particular interest to us today is the fact that the language used by Romans to describe the nature and work of the emperors was reminiscent of language that Judaism used for God and that the church used for Jesus. For example, an inscription on a monument to the emperor Augustus calls the emperor the beginning of all things, the savior who has become god manifest whose reign is good news (gospel). Various emperors were known by the titles savior, son of god, and lord.[2] Furthermore, shrines were erected to many of the emperors at key places in the empire. Given the Roman context, when the church used similar language about Jesus, that language was obviously intended to show that Jesus is the trustworthy representative of the living God whereas the emperor was an idolater. The realm of God would be unimaginably greater than the rule of the emperor, and not despoiled like that of the emperor.

Christians today sometimes have the mistaken impression that Jewish and Gentile peoples lived in completely separate spheres and despised one another. A more accurate picture is that a significant number of Gentiles lived in the Holy Land, and for the most part Jewish and Gentile peoples lived alongside one another and often peacefully. Day-to-day survival could be difficult for both Jewish and Gentile peoples, especially for those in the lower levels of the economic and social pyramid.

A Key Question for Jewish People

The pressures of hellenization in the Holy Land began with Alexander and continued for several centuries. Although governments changed, the pressure on local peoples to adapt to the hellenization continued. People in each nation around the Mediterranean basin faced this key question: How do we respond to hellenization? They had three choices.

- Do we simply accept it and become as hellenized as possible?
- Do we try to maintain the core identity of our own culture while learning to live with hellenization?
- Do we reject hellenization?

These questions had been critical for the Jewish community since Alexander's time. By Alexander's death, most of the First Testament had been written.* But the First Testament did not provide clear, direct guidance. Consequently, Jewish people were in active conversation with one another (sometimes disagreeing) throughout the Hellenistic Age regarding how to respond to hellenization.

For Jewish communities, the issues were not simply how much of their own cultural identity they could surrender to hellenization and its intensification in Roman occupation. The issue was one of faithfulness. How much could they adapt to hellenization and still remain faithful? Similar questions still trouble Jewish communities today, and Christian congregations, denominations, and movements as well.

Judaisms in the World of Jesus

A friend who read through this manuscript crossed out the "s" at the end of "Judaisms" in the subtitle of this section and said, "You mean Judaism (singular)." In a broad sense, of course, we could speak of Judaism (singular), but using the plural (Judaisms) calls attention to the existence of diverse expressions of Judaism in the Hellenistic Age. Christians should seldom speak of *the* Jewish attitude toward a particular issue but should take into account the fact that on particular matters different Jewish groups often had different perspectives. The different strands of Judaism offered different theological responses to hellenization. We may distinguish six groups.

First, the Sadducees were an upper-class group (who included the priestly party) who often cooperated with the Romans, thereby profiting from the Roman economic system and maintaining their own

---

* The First Testament, or Old Testament, is sometimes today called the Hebrew Bible, the Prime Testament, or the Torah, Prophets, and Writings. The Second Testament, or New Testament, is sometimes called the Greek Testament or the Gospels and Letters.

power. Indeed, as noted earlier, the role of chief priest sometimes included that of civil official. The Sadducees regarded only the first five books of the Bible as their theological authorities. Since those books do not teach the resurrection of the dead, the Sadducees did not accept that doctrine. We hear these themes in the description of the Sadducees by Josephus, a first-century CE Jewish writer.

> The Sadducees hold that the soul perishes along with the body. They own no observance of any sort apart from the laws [i.e., the written law]; in fact, they reckon it a virtue to dispute with the teachers of the path of wisdom that they pursue. There are but few [people] to whom this doctrine has been made known, but these are [people] of the highest standing. They accomplish practically nothing, however. For whenever they assume some office, though they submit unwillingly and perforce, yet submit they do to the formulas of the Pharisees, since otherwise the masses would not tolerate them.[3]

Second, of all ancient Jewish groups, the Pharisees are most famil-iar to many Christians today. The Pharisees responded to hellenization by trying to encourage the Jewish community to maintain its distinc-tive identity while making its way in a relatively benign way through the occupation through personal obedience and faithfulness. Because I discuss the Pharisees extensively in chapter 4, I mention them only briefly here. Although many contemporary Christians think the Phar-isees were a large and legalistic group, there were only a few thousand of them in antiquity, and contrary to the popular picture today, they were a reform movement in Judaism that called for obedience to Torah in everyday life as a joyous response to a gracious and loving God.

Third, the Essenes lived on the edge of the Dead Sea at a place known as Qumran. The Essenes were largely apocalyptic in orienta-tion, believing that God was about to destroy the present evil world and replace it with a new righteous one (see remarks about apocalyp-ticism immediately below). The Essenes moved to the Dead Sea as an act of withdrawing from the mainstream of society to await the new world in the wilderness where, according to Isaiah 40:3, they expected it to begin. Josephus describes these and other characteristic Essene beliefs and practices as follows.

The doctrine of the Essenes is wont to leave everything in the hands of God. They regard the soul as immortal and believe that they ought to strive especially to draw near to righteousness. They send votive offerings to the temple, but perform their sacrifices employing a different ritual of purification. For this reason they are barred from those precincts of the people that are frequented by all the people and perform their rites by themselves. Otherwise they are of the highest character, devoting themselves solely to agricultural labor. They deserve admiration in contrast to all others who claim their share of virtue because such qualities as theirs were never found among any Greek or barbarian people, nay, not even briefly, but have been among them in constant practice and never interrupted since they adopted them from of old. Moreover, they hold their possessions in common, and the wealthy [person] receives no more enjoyment from . . . property than the [one] who possesses nothing. The number of men who practice this way of life number more than four thousand. They neither bring their wives into community nor do they own slaves, since they believe that the latter practice contributes to injustice and that the former opens the way to a source of dissension. Instead they live by themselves and perform menial tasks for one another. They elect by show of hands good men to receive their revenues and the produce of the earth and priests to prepare bread and other food.[4]

Some scholars think that John the Baptist had a connection to the Essene community. John was certainly apocalyptic, but it is not certain he had a direct relationship to the Essenes.

Fourth, apocalyptic visionaries held views that were related to the Essenes, but many of these prophets did not withdraw from the world. This viewpoint is discussed more fully in the first part of chapter 3. For now it is enough to note that the apocalyptists believed that God would end the present evil age and replace it with a new one by means of a massive historical interruption (an apocalypse). They expected God to be the primary actor in this event; the human role was to repent and remain faithful. John the Baptist was such an apocalyptic preacher (Matt. 3:1–12; Mark 1:2–8; Luke 3:1–20).

A fifth group, the Zealots, proposed armed resistance to Roman domination. The Zealots believed that God would turn a revolt into a

Holy War in which God fought through them. Here is how Josephus describes the Zealots.

> This school agrees in all other respects with the opinions of the Pharisees except that they have a passion for liberty that is almost unconquerable, since they are convinced that God alone is their leader and master. They think little of submitting to death in unusual forms and permitting vengeance to fall on kinsmen and friends if only they may avoid calling any [human being] master. Inasmuch as most people have seen the steadfastness of their resolution amid such circumstances, I may forgo any further account. For I hear that anything reported of them will be considered incredible. The danger is, rather, that report may minimize the indifference with which they accept the grinding misery of pain.[5]

Simon, one of Jesus' disciples, belonged to the Zealots (Luke 6:15; Acts 1:13).

The sixth contingent, the people of the land, comprised the largest number of Jewish residents of the land of Israel and was not organized as a distinct party. Indeed, they did not strongly align themselves with the other parties. Apparently many people of the land sought to be faithful Jewish people. Few were driven by a distinct agenda other than to survive economically. Many were poor, living on small plots of land or working for a daily wage. Many were ready for the occupation to end. A good many held to a popular apocalyptic hope for God to end the present age and replace it with a new one.

Questions for Discussion

1. Can you name three ideas in this chapter regarding life in the land of Israel at the time of Jesus that are new to you or that strike you with fresh force?
2. Can you describe forces in the world today that are similar to hellenization in antiquity, that is, forces that put pressure on local communities and cultures to move away from some of their distinct, local values and practices and to embrace more general ones?

3. As you think about Christians that you know—individuals, congregations, denominations, and movements—which ones seem to respond to the world today in ways similar to the following: (a) Sadducees, (b) Pharisees, (c) Essenes, (d) other apocalyptic thinkers, (e) Zealots, (f) people of the land?
4. What do you see as strengths and weaknesses of the approach of each group listed in question 3, both in antiquity and today?
5. At this point in your study, with which of the groups in question 3 do you least identify? Most identify? Why?

3

The Realm of God:
Focus of the Ministry of Jesus

*T*he reader might expect a book on the life of Jesus to begin with his birth. In documents from the Greek and Roman worlds, however, the first and last words spoken by a character often provide important information regarding how to interpret that character. In Mark, Matthew, and Luke, the first words that Jesus spoke at the beginning of his public ministry reveal the purpose of that ministry and provide a framework for understanding everything he says and does in the first three Gospels.

In Mark, Jesus launches his ministry by declaring, "The time is fulfilled, and the [realm] of God has come near; repent, and believe in the good news" (Mark 1:15). For Mark, the notion of the realm of God interprets the ministry of Jesus. Matthew offers a simpler version of the same theme, "Repent, for the [realm] of heaven has come near" (Matt. 4:17).* While Luke does not directly use the words *realm of God*, the language and imagery of Jesus' inaugural sermon at Nazareth signals that the ministry of Jesus is focused on realm (Luke 4:16–30).

Most English translations of the Bible speak of the kingdom of God rather than the realm of God. Many people today find the term *kingdom* unsatisfactory because it is unnecessarily gender-specific by implying that God is male and indirectly licensing male superiority. Many Christians today note that the Bible itself contains feminine images for God and that apocalyptic literature sees the life in Eden (including egalitarianism between

---

* Matthew uses the phrase "realm of heaven" instead of "realm of God." These expressions are different ways of saying the same thing.

women and men) as the pattern for life in the realm. The word *realm* better captures this spirit than does the term *kingdom*.[1]

What Did Jesus Mean by the Realm of God?

In the ancient world, a realm was a particular place at a particular time shaped by particular values and activities. To speak of the realm of God is to refer to the specific time and place where life takes place according to God's purposes. What does the expression *realm of God* mean in Jesus' context? How did Jesus expect it to come?

Scholars fall into two large schools (with many different nuances within each) regarding how Jesus used the term *realm of God*. The interpretation I find convincing is from the school that holds that Jesus articulated an apocalyptic vision of the realm. This approach is convincing because its main lines were commonplace in antiquity, which makes Jesus a person of his own time. Furthermore, it permeates the books of Mark, Matthew, and Luke. While the Gospel writers emphasize different perspectives on the realm, it is logical to think that their commonly shared apocalyptic core echoes Jesus himself.

The other school holds that Jesus was nonapocalyptic. This way of thinking is especially associated today with the Jesus Seminar, but many other scholars share it.[2] This school holds that Jesus envisioned the realm as an altogether present phenomenon. Some interpreters in this stream think that Jesus actively opposed first-century apocalyptic thinking. Some scholars within this school think that Jesus envisioned the realm not as an ongoing social or cosmic reality but as coming to expression in occasional moments that embody the values of the realm. I once heard someone describe this version of the realm as occurring "here and there, now and then." I do not find this way of interpreting the historical Jesus persuasive because this picture of Jesus would have been out of place in the first century. In fact, this viewpoint sounds like anachronism—contemporary people who do not like the apocalyptic viewpoint retrojecting onto Jesus their own way of perceiving God's activity in the world. This way of thinking seems to me a way of getting a Jesus that we like (see my remarks on this subject in chap. 1).

The Apocalyptic Meaning of Realm of God

Apocalyptic thinking was a commonplace Jewish phenomenon at the time of Jesus. Dozens of documents with an apocalyptic flavor were circulating with names such as 2 Esdras, *1 Enoch*, *2 Baruch*, and the *Testaments of the Twelve Patriarchs*. Apocalyptic documents were as capable of being understood in that time as religious books are today.[3]

While proto-apocalyptic elements appear in Isaiah 56–66 and in Zechariah 9–12, apocalyptic thinking appears in a fully developed form in the First Testament only in Daniel 7–12 (written about 168–165 BCE). Apocalyptic thinking emerged in the Jewish community during the Hellenistic Age as Jewish teachers sought two things: (1) a theological explanation for why the world was so difficult, and (2) a rationale for hope, for being able to live with confidence through the fractious experience of the world. The pastoral purpose of this literature is to help the community endure.

Apocalypticism became particularly attractive during the Roman occupation. Some apocalyptic writings (e.g., the book of Revelation) regard the empire as the social embodiment of evil. People today sometimes mindlessly criticize apocalypticism as "pie in the sky bye and bye," but this literature was born in the crucible of human suffering as a way to make sense of the experience of suffering and as reason for living in hope.

A foundational element in apocalyptic theology is that God has always had and will always have sovereign control over all things. In heaven, everything already reflects God's purposes. In the world, nothing happens apart from God's direct initiative or God's permission. In this sense, God already and always rules. However, the world in its present state does not fully embody the quality of life that God desires.

First Era: The World as Eden

While the apocalyptic thinkers were diverse regarding details, they generally thought of history as divided into four eras. The first is the world in Genesis 1–2, when all elements of creation lived together according to God's purposes as a community of mutual support. This world had no sickness, injustice, oppression, violence, or death, and it was a time of egalitarianism between the man and the woman, as well as harmony between humankind and nature. The world remained an Eden as long as the people respected the boundaries and purposes that God set for them. This period is very important to apocalyptic thinkers because they anticipate that the end times (the fully developed realm) would be like the beginning times. The Gospels contain indications that Jesus understood the time of creation in this way. In the midst of a controversy about divorce, for instance, Jesus refers to the relationship of Adam and Eve as the pattern God intended for women and men, whereas after the fall Moses allowed divorce as a concession to hardness of heart (Mark 10:2–9; Matt. 19:1–9).

Second Era: The Present Evil Age

The second era began with the fall. According to some apocalyptic authors, Satan came to Adam and Eve in the form of the snake and urged them to transgress the boundaries God had set, and thereby to acquire power and knowledge that were meant only for God (Gen. 3:1–13). When the first couple yielded to this temptation, God cursed them. Henceforth, women would feel pain in childbearing and would be subservient to men. For men, labor would become a burden. Death would be the final destination of every life. God even cursed the relationship of humankind and nature (Gen. 3:14–19).

Life in this second era (sometimes known as the old age, the old creation, the present evil age, or the realm of this world) would be marked by the presence of Satan and demons exercising power that deformed life, as well as by idolatry, arrogance, oppression, injustice, exploitation, poverty, sickness, enmity between humankind and nature, violence, and death. Jewish theologians perceived these conditions intensifying in the time of hellenization and especially during the Roman occupation.

The circumstance of the old age raised an important theological question for Jewish teachers. How would God end this oppressive situation? What would God do to be faithful to God's promises to bless the human family? They answered this question by posing the idea of an apocalypse followed by a new age as demonstrating the trustworthiness of God and as giving the believing community reason to endure the present and to live toward the future with hope.

Third Era: Tribulation and Apocalypse

The third era is the time leading up to the apocalypse and the apocalypse itself. Apocalyptic thinkers reasoned that God had decided very long ago the date when the apocalypse would occur. This idea may seem arbitrary to people today but it was an ancient way of asserting divine control over all events as a way of believing that history would not become chaos. Prior to the apocalypse, Satan and the demons would intensify the suffering of the world, especially the suffering of the faithful, in order to dissuade people from turning to God. This period is sometimes called the tribulation.

At the moment of the apocalypse, God or God's representatives (such as angels) would come from heaven and defeat Satan and his minions. After a savage battle, God would end the power of Satan and would finally and fully manifest the realm. God would bring to life all people who had lived previously (resurrection) and would judge everyone, welcoming the faithful into the realm but consigning the unfaithful to punishment.

Fourth Era: Realm of God

The fourth era is the post-apocalypse world, when the realm of God is present in its fullness.* The realm restores humankind and nature. In the new age, God's purposes shape every individual, relationship, and situation. The realm is one of justice, mutuality, abundance, health, and blessing between humankind and nature. People have transformed bodies, resurrection bodies that are no longer subject to decay and death. A passage from the apocalyptic book of *1 Enoch* represents many other descriptions of the world to come.

---

* The realm of God is sometimes called the new age, the new creation, or the world to come.

And in those days the whole earth will be worked in righteousness, all of her planted with trees, and will find blessing. And
they shall plant pleasant trees upon her—vines. And [the one
who] plants a vine upon [the earth] will produce wine for plen-
itude. And every seed that is sown on [the earth], one measure
will yield a thousand (measures), and one measure of olives will
yield ten measures of presses of oil. And you cleanse the earth
from all injustice and from all defilement, and from all oppression, and from all sin, and from all iniquity which is being done
on earth; remove them from the earth. And all the children of the
people will become righteous, and all nations shall worship and
bless me; and they will all prostrate themselves to me. And the
earth shall be cleansed from all pollution, and from all sin, and
from all plague, and from all suffering; and it shall not happen
again that I shall send (these) upon the earth from generation to
generation and forever. (*1 En.* 10:18–22)[4]

The realm promised not only release from Roman occupation but the
regeneration of all sectors of life. The coming of the realm demonstrates that God is faithful and trustworthy. By giving them life in the
new creation, the coming of the realm shows that God acts justly
toward the faithful who died amid the tensions of the old age. This
hope makes endurance worth it.

Present and Future of the Realm
in the Ministry of Jesus

As noted at the beginning of this chapter, Jesus interpreted his ministry
as announcing that the final manifestation of the realm is about to
occur. His purpose was to announce that the apocalypse was near, with
its twin dimensions of destruction of the old world and construction of
the new. Jesus urged people to prepare through repentance.

Jesus and his followers add two elements to Jewish understanding
of the realm. These new elements have to do with the role of Jesus and
the timing of the event. Paul and the first three Gospels present Jesus
as God's agent for the final manifestation of the realm. At one level,
Jesus is not only an apocalyptic prophet who announces the coming
of the realm but is an active agent in bringing it. Paul and the Gospel

writers presumed that after the resurrection Jesus ascended to heaven and would return from heaven. Indeed, the return of Jesus would be the apocalypse (e.g., 1 Thess. 4:13–5:11; 1 Cor. 15:20–28; Mark 13:24–27; Matt. 24:29–31; and Luke 21:2–28).

Paul and the Gospel writers also reconfigured the timing of the apocalypse. For Paul and for the authors of Mark, Matthew, and Luke the coming of the realm is not entirely future; instead, aspects of the realm already come to expression within present history. Scholars sometimes speak of this phenomenon as the "already and not-yet" of the realm. Elements of the realm are already at work, but the realm is not yet altogether here. A scholar in a previous generation compared this situation to the relationship between D-day and the liberation of Europe in World War II. The landing of the allied forces at Normandy on D-day signaled the defeat of the Nazi grip on Europe. The invasion promised final victory, although that victory was almost a year away.[5]

For Paul, the cross and the resurrection are the turning point of the ages. The resurrection of Jesus anticipates the general resurrection expected at the apocalypse, thus showing that the power of the coming world is already at work in the present, although on a limited basis. Mark understands the in-breaking of the realm to begin with the baptism of Jesus (Mark 1:9–11). Mathew and Luke each interpret the coming of the apocalyptic age as beginning with the birth of Jesus.

Paul and the writers of the first three Gospels portray the intensification of suffering in the last days as taking place in their own times. In a poignant passage Paul says that "the whole creation has been groaning in labor pains until now; and not only the creation, but we ourselves, who have the first fruits of the Spirit, groan inwardly while we wait for adoption, the redemption of our bodies" (Rom. 8:22–23). Mark, Matthew, and Luke were written after the Romans destroyed the temple in 70 CE and left the nation in chaos. The Gospel writers see the chaos after the destruction of the temple as part of the intense suffering (tribulation) expected right before the apocalypse (Mark 13:1–23, 28–37; Matt. 24:1–28, 32–34; Luke 21:5–24, 29–36).

Although the Gospel writers expected Jesus to return fairly soon, they did not to try to pinpoint the day or time. Indeed, in Mark and Matthew, Jesus says, "But about that day or hour no one knows, neither the angels in heaven, nor the Son, but only the Father" (Mark 13:32;

Matt. 24:36). Luke expected the second coming in the foreseeable future but also anticipated a delay in its arrival (e.g., Luke 21:32–33).

Realm as Lens for the Ministry of Jesus

In Mark, Matthew, and Luke the realm is used as a lens through which to interpret all of Jesus' ministry. His preaching alerts people to the coming of the realm. His teaching explains how to live in response to it. His actions (e.g., miracles and table fellowship) embody it. The Gospels picture some people opposing his interpretation of the realm and creating conflict with him. God raised Jesus from the dead as definitive demonstration of the presence and coming of the realm. We explore these dimensions in chapters 4–9.

Major Questions for Today's Church

On the one hand, this perspective on the realm as renewed social and cosmic world appeals to many people in the early twenty-first century, since our world has many old-age qualities such as social fractiousness, poverty, hunger for meaning in life, the search for authentic community, the prospect of environmental catastrophe, and manifold forms of violence and death. We would like to believe that the realm is operating among us. Preachers often lift up realm-like moments that take place in life around us to encourage congregations and urge listeners to join those moments as they unfold.

On the other hand, it has been almost two thousand years since Jesus announced that the realm was soon to arrive in its fullness, but it still has not come. We can respond to this situation in one of two ways. First, we can view it as a delay and can surmise that we do not have an adequate understanding of God's time line for the apocalypse. I would like to have a dollar for each time I have heard a Christian echo the saying "With God, one day is like a thousand years, and a thousand years are like one day" (see Ps. 90:4; 2 Pet. 3:8). Perhaps Jesus himself misunderstood God's time line. We do not know when the apocalypse will occur, but we should look for its signs now and its eventual coming in fullness. Or, we can conclude that an apocalypse is not likely to occur. The many people who adopt this viewpoint then face the question of what they can believe regarding God's ultimate purposes for the world. I return to these questions in chapter 12.

Questions for Discussion

1. Before reading this chapter, what associations (if any) did you have with the notion of the realm of God? How does the perspective of this chapter compare with your previous thinking about the realm?
2. Where do you see attitudes and behaviors in the world today that demonstrate characteristics of the old age?
3. Where do you see events today that anticipate the realm of God in personal lives, households, social situations, and political development?
4. The apocalyptic return of Jesus on the clouds has not taken place. At the present time, do you believe that Jesus will return in the way pictured in Mark, Matthew, and Luke? If not, what *do* you believe about God's ultimate purposes for human community and the earth?

4

The Birth of Jesus and the Beginning of His Ministry

*B*ible students often note that Paul had little interest in the sayings and stories from the life of Jesus. Mark does not tell the story of the birth of Jesus but begins with the baptism of Jesus. Both Matthew and Luke begin with stories of the birth of Jesus. The Gospel of John opens not with the birth of Jesus but with Jesus in the presence of God before creation.

Less commonly noticed is the reason for these differences: the different New Testament writers locate the beginning of the final manifestation of the realm of God at different times. Paul dates the final manifestation as beginning at Jesus' death and resurrection. Mark moves the turning point to the baptism. Matthew and Luke make it even sooner by interpreting the birth as signaling the final revelation of the realm. John's understanding of the world and of the purpose of Jesus is quite different (see chap. 10).

Two Birth Stories: Matthew and Luke

The church today is in a strange situation with respect to the birth of Jesus. Christmas is one of the two biggest seasons for the church, often arousing more energy than Easter. Yet the birth of Jesus takes up a tiny portion of only two Gospels.[1] The other writers of the Second Testament have no interest in the birth of Jesus per se.

Most scholars think that the stories of the birth of Jesus are not biographical reports that could be featured in a documentary but were shaped in Matthew and Luke to establish the identity of Jesus and to introduce themes that are important in these Gospels. We speak not of *the* birth of Jesus but of *the two stories* of the birth of Jesus. We should not harmonize these stories into one as many congregations do on Christmas Eve, but should honor the integrity of each by looking at the stories one at a time.

In fact, neither Matthew nor Luke presents a virgin *birth* but rather a virginal *conception*. People in antiquity often told stories of special qualities surrounding the births of major figures in order to establish the credibility of the figures: from the outset, the gods were guiding people born in this way. Several groups in the ancient world narrated virginal conceptions of their leading figures. The stories of the birth of Jesus show that his life and mission were authorized by God.

If Mary and Joseph were preparing to marry at the usual ages in antiquity, they would have been in their early to middle teen years. The date December 25 is nowhere mentioned in the Bible but was adapted by the church from a Roman sun festival at least two centuries after the birth of Jesus.

Matthew: God with Us, Insightful Pagan Astrologers, and Evil Herod

Matthew 1:18–25 interprets the identity of Jesus as Emmanuel, "God is with us." Matthew derives the meaning "God is with us" from Isaiah 7:14 (see Isa. 7:1–25). Isaiah spoke to the nation of Judah. Ahaz, ruler of Judah, was in a complex situation. In order to stave off invasion by the giant Assyria, two small nations to the north of Judah proposed an alliance with Judah. When Ahaz hesitated to join the alliance, the two nations threatened to invade Judah and depose Ahaz to force Judah into the alliance.

Ahaz was torn between joining the alliance and asking Assyria for help against the two nations. Isaiah counseled Ahaz to do neither but to trust that God would protect Judah. Indeed, Isaiah said that God would confirm this promise to Ahaz by performing any sign that Ahaz chose. When Ahaz refused to make a choice, Isaiah pointed to a young woman who was pregnant who would name her child Immanuel (Isa. 7:14). The life of the child would be a sign of salvation and judgment. Before the child reached the age of distinguishing right from wrong, the alliance would not conquer Judah (salvation) but soon Judah would fall to Assyria (judgment) (Isa. 7:14–25).

By using Isaiah 7:14, Matthew indicates that Jesus is a sign of the times similar to the birth of the child in the days of Isaiah. From Matthew's apocalyptic perspective, the ministry, death, and resurrection of Jesus is a sign of the final manifestation of the realm and the accompanying judgment.

We confuse the identity of the visitors from the East in Matthew 2:1–12 by calling them "kings" or "wise ones." Matthew presents them as pagan astrologers who read the stars because they believed that the stars revealed important events (such as the births of important figures). The astrologers are Gentiles, and Matthew uses them to prefigure Gentiles recognizing the work of the God of Israel through Jesus. Matthew does not directly say how many astrologers came to the house where Jesus was born. Later Christians began to speak of three because they brought three gifts.

Herod (a local client-ruler employed by the Romans) sought to kill Jesus because the astrologers identified Jesus as ruler of the Jews (Matt. 2:2, 13–18). Herod perceived Jesus as a threat to the peace and perhaps even as a challenge to Herod's own rule. When Herod could not ascertain where Jesus was born, Herod ordered the murder of all the children around Bethlehem, supposing that Jesus would be killed in the process. Matthew's depiction of Herod's brutality in 2:13–23 presents a picture of the nature of political rule in the old age and of the Roman governmental system in particular. Readers expect civil rulers in this Gospel to behave like Herod (e.g., Matt. 14:1–12; 27:11–26) and are surprised when occasional Romans respond more like the pagan astrologers (Matt. 8:5–13). Matthew uses this picture of Herod as a pastoral warning to his congregation to be wary of civil authorities. Witnessing to the realm can bring people into conflict with such rulers.

At the same time, this part of Matthew's Gospel dramatizes God's power and providence in directing the life of Jesus. An angel warns the Holy Family to flee to Egypt, where they are safe. When Herod dies, they return safely to Nazareth (Matt. 2:19–23). Such providence continues throughout Jesus' witness to the realm during his ministry and is definitively revealed when Jesus is raised from the dead. Matthew wants his community to believe that a similar providence supports them as they witness to the realm amid conflicts of their own time.

Luke: Mary as Model, Shepherds, and Circumcision (Jewish Authenticity)

In Luke, too, the birth of Jesus takes place in a Jewish milieu. The first event in the Gospel is in the temple. The parents of John the Baptist are a priest (Zechariah) and a faithful Jewish woman (Elizabeth). Zechariah does not initially grasp the significance of John's birth, and God makes him unable to speak. By contrast, the woman (Elizabeth) immediately understands the event and responds as God wants (Luke 1:5–25).

Scholars frequently describe Mary as a model of faithfulness in Luke-Acts. When she is a young virgin engaged to Joseph, the angel Gabriel announces to her that the Holy Spirit will overshadow her so that she will conceive a child who will be an instrument in establishing the realm (Luke 1:26–38). Mary immediately accepts. Her attitude and behavior presage a theme in Luke-Acts: women tend to be models of discipleship. Luke would like for all who receive the message of the realm to respond as Mary does.

Mary is the first human character in the Gospel of Luke to point to the final materialization of the realm when she utters a speech known as "the Magnificat" (from the opening phrase, "My soul magnifies the Lord"). Mary describes the social world in the realm: shaped by God's mercy (a term that echoes the famous Hebrew term *hesed*—covenantal loyalty, steadfast love, loving-kindness), the end of brutal rule, redistribution of social power, upgrading the situation of people in the lower social order, provision for the hungry, safety for Israel (Luke 1:46–55).

Luke's first direct reference to Rome alludes to the empire's oppression by noting that the birth of Jesus took place at the time of a registration that would facilitate taxation (Luke 2:1–4). The reader understands Rome as among the proud and powerful that will be brought down. However, Luke recognizes that God can use Rome for providence (e.g., Romans rescue Paul from danger in Acts 23:12–35).

Luke places the newborn Jesus in a manger (a feeding trough or a stall) because there was "no place for them in the inn." The word "inn" can refer to something like an early motel, or to a room that some houses had for guests, or to the sleeping part of a one-room house (Luke 2:5–7). That the world had no adequate place for Jesus points to its broken character and the need for the realm.

Angels make the first public announcement of the birth to shepherds (Luke 2:7–20). Scholars point out that the birth of Caesar was sometimes described as "good news," the same language used in Luke 2:10. Luke thus pushes people to consider the question, Which is the true good news for the world—the rule of Caesar or the rule of God?

Although we tend to romanticize shepherds today, in antiquity shepherds were regarded as lower class, dirty, and antisocial, and with suspicion. Jacob, after all, stole Laban's best sheep (Gen. 30:25–43). Luke uses the announcement to the shepherds to make an important point: the realm will renew the entire social world. By the end of the book of Acts, the good news that comes first to shepherds (at the bottom of the social pyramid) has made its way to high officials in the Roman Empire and even to Rome itself (Acts 21:17–28:31). All who repent (see below) are welcome in the realm.

Joseph and Mary have Jesus circumcised (the quintessential sign of Jewish identity) and carry out other rites (Luke 2:21–24). The prophet Simeon confirms that Jesus will manifest a realm that includes Gentiles. Yet the witness to the realm will create conflict (Luke 2:25–35). The prophetess Anna also speaks positively about Jesus (Luke 2:36–38). Jesus so matured in the knowledge of God that at the age of twelve Jesus taught in the temple (Luke 2:39–51).

Luke uses the story of the birth of Jesus to establish that Jesus and the mission that follows from him are authentically Jewish. The God of Israel is responsible for his birth. His uncle was a priest. A prophet and prophetess approved. He was circumcised. At the age of twelve, he was a teacher. As the story of Jesus and his followers unfolds in the Gospel of Luke and the book of Acts, we are to hear this narrative (especially the welcome of Gentiles in Acts) as an extension of the story that began in the First Testament and will be complete only at the final manifestation of the realm.

The Baptism of Jesus

Most scholars agree that Jesus was baptized by John the Baptist. The first three Gospels all portray John as an apocalyptic preacher announcing that God would soon end the present age with an apocalypse and would then bring about the realm (Mark 1:1–8; Matt. 3:1–12; Luke 3:1–20). John urged people to prepare for the change by repenting and by being baptized (probably by immersion). Repentance was a positive and dynamic action meaning to turn away from complicity with Satan, the demons, and the old age, and to turn toward God and the realm. For both Matthew and Luke, the repentant life is one lived according to the values and behaviors of the realm in the present (e.g., through sharing material resources and living justly, Matt. 3:7–10; Luke 3:7–14). Matthew and Luke agree that the apocalypse would be accompanied by a fiery punishment for the nonrepentant (Matt. 3:11–12; Luke 3:1–18). For John the Baptist, baptism was both a sign of repentance and a mark of belonging to the community of the new age.

By being baptized by John, Jesus identified himself as sharing John's apocalyptic perspective. Both John and Jesus believed that the apocalypse was imminent. The differences between John and Jesus were of timing and agency. John pointed to the coming of the apocalypse as an altogether future event. The Gospels portray the realm as becoming partially manifest through the present ministry of Jesus (with the full manifestation to come in the near future) and Jesus as an instrument in its coming.

Each detail of the baptism of Jesus is significant. It took place in the River Jordan. Because Joshua and the tribes of Israel entered the promised land by crossing the Jordan, that river functions as a symbol of crossing from an old life into a new (Josh. 3:1–4:24). The heavens opened, something that the apocalyptic writers since Isaiah expected as part of the final manifestation of the realm (Isa. 64:1). The outpouring of the Spirit was expected to intensify in the last days and in the realm (e.g., Joel 2:28–29). Because Noah sent the dove from the ark to see whether the flood had subsided so that the new life on the earth could begin (Gen. 8:6–12), the presence of the dove signals that the time has come for the regeneration of the earth.

God spoke from heaven, "You are my Son, the Beloved; with you I am well pleased" (Mark 1:11). The voice from heaven combined parts of Psalm 2:7 and Isaiah 42:1. Psalm 2 was sung in Israel when a prince was crowned monarch and took the throne to reign. Psalm 2:7 indicates that on the coronation day, God adopted the monarch as God's own heir and agent. The monarch in Israel was to guide the community in living according to covenantal love and justice (e.g., Ps. 72). Isaiah 42:1–9 is the first of four "Servant Songs" in Isaiah that identify the call and mission of Israel. The community is to be a light to the Gentiles (Isa. 42:6); that is, to model how God wants all peoples to live together in justice. The Servant suffers carrying out this mission. The Gospel writers thus certify that Jesus is God's agent who is instrumental in bringing the realm (much like the Servant), although Jesus operates with an apocalyptic agenda.

The story of the baptism of Jesus evidently functioned in the early communities of Jesus' followers as a model of how baptism was to function for them. When people were baptized, they were marked and claimed for the community of witnesses to the realm.

The Temptation of Jesus

After the baptism Jesus was tempted by Satan (the devil). As noted previously, many Jewish authors anticipated an intense period of suffering (the tribulation) shortly before the end. During that time, people would be tempted to abandon God and to turn to other authorities in the hope of easing their suffering. Mark implies that the temptation of Jesus was a miniature of this period of difficulty in which Jesus experienced a face-to-face confrontation with Satan (Mark 1:12–13). The Spirit drove Jesus into the wilderness to demonstrate that God was taking the initiative in bringing the realm.

In the First Testament, Satan is a member of God's court who works for God (e.g., Job 1:1–2:12; Zech. 3:1–2). In the Hellenistic Age, however, Jewish apocalyptic writers began to portray Satan as an opponent of God who had such extraordinary power that Satan ruled the old age. God would end Satan's reign. Satan is the power behind the great tribulation.

Matthew and Luke expand the story of the temptation to include three specific temptations (Matt. 4:1–11; Luke 4:1–13). However, they order the temptations differently.

Matthew	**Luke**
1. Turn stones into bread	1. Turn stones into bread
2. Jump off pinnacle of temple	2. Rule dominions of world
3. Rule dominions of world	3. Jump off pinnacle of temple

The temptation to turn stones into bread assumed that bread is necessary for life. The temptation is to turn elsewhere rather than to trust God for bread in the tribulation. With respect to the temptation to jump off a high tower at the temple into the arms of angels, the readers knew the temple had been besieged by the Romans. Leaping into the arms of angels would avoid the suffering of the last age represented by the destruction of the temple. The other temptation was idolatry: to worship Satan and thereby to become ruler of the realms of the old age. Jesus, however, was called not to replace Rome as ruler of existing realms but to bring the realm of God. The suffering of the last days was unavoidable, because the apocalypse means the destruction of the old age before the new can come. To try to escape this difficult period is to yield to Satan.

Jesus resists temptation. The story of the temptation has a double function. It demonstrates that Jesus is a reliable guide through the chaos prior to the apocalypse. For Jesus faced Satan and did not yield. And it is a model for Jesus' followers. In the power of the Spirit, they too can resist Satan in the great suffering of the last days.

The Initial Preaching of Jesus

Each of the first three Gospels begins by presenting Jesus as agent of the realm. It is not surprising, then, as we note at the beginning of chapter 3, that these Gospels present his first public words as announcing that the realm will soon be fully manifest (Mark 1:14–15; Matt. 4:12–17; Luke 4:14–30).

Questions for Discussion

1. Recall the most recent Christmas Eve services in your congregation. Do they harmonize (or meld together) the birth stories of Matthew and Luke, and the beginning of the Gospel of John? Think about how your congregation might develop a Christmas pageant or Christmas Eve service focused on only one Gospel.
2. Who would you identify today as people who are similar to the astrologers, that is, people who are outside the household of faith but who have insight into God's purposes?
3. Name women in your congregation or in the larger world who, like Mary, demonstrate faithful discipleship by stepping outside the usual roles assumed by women.
4. How does the explanation of the baptism of Jesus in this chapter compare and contrast with your understanding of baptism? With the teaching about baptism in your church?
5. Where do you and your congregation experience temptation today? How do you experience the Spirit's presence, helping you resist?

Jesus, Judaism, and Conflict with Others

Jesus was Jewish. He participated in Judaism in his time as a faithful Jew. He understood his movement as one within Judaism whose purpose was to witness to a realm that would eventually embrace Jewish and Gentile peoples. While such statements may seem obvious today, there have been periods in the church when Christians viewed Jesus as alien to Judaism. Some Christians have portrayed Jesus as seeking to renew Judaism, or as rejecting Judaism, and as aiming to replace Judaism with Christianity. Indeed, some Christians hold such ideas today.

This chapter explores some indications of Jesus' Jewishness. We also examine stories in which Jesus is portrayed as being in conflict with other Jewish leaders. I conclude that such stories are caricatures with the unfortunate consequence of reinforcing anti-Judaism today. A part of the mission of the church today is to renounce such stories.

Indications of the Jewishness of Jesus

The Gospels describe several aspects of the life of Jesus that were typical of Jewish culture in the first century CE. The Gospel writers (who wrote after 70 CE) saw the future of the Jesus movement as moving toward Gentiles, and so they had reason to play down the Jewish background of Jesus. The fact that the Gospel writers preserved some of these details when they did not need to do so gives the details a significant claim to historicity. It was important to these authors to picture Jesus as a faithful Jew.

Jesus' *name* is the first sign of his Jewishness. The name Jesus (which was fairly common in Jewish circles in the first century) is a Greek form of the Hebrew name Joshua and means "God saves," thus indicating that the story of Jesus is a continuation of the story of God's saving work from the First Testament. The names of people closely associated with Jesus were Jewish. For example, the names Mary and Joseph reflect characters in the First Testament. (Mary is a Greek form of Miriam, the name of Moses' sister.) Although the lists of the twelve disciples are not the same in all three Gospels, the names of the twelve were Jewish (e.g., Mark 3:13–19; Matt. 10:1–4; Luke 6:12–16).

The *birth of Jesus* is depicted as taking place in a faithful Jewish atmosphere. His parents and relatives were Jewish, and according to Luke, he was circumcised and raised in the Jewish manner so that at the age of twelve he joined the adults in the temple.

The life of Jesus took place largely *in the land of Israel*. Bethlehem, Nazareth, Capernaum, the Sea of Galilee, Bethany, Jerusalem—these places had significant Jewish populations and were Jewish in culture. When the Gospels picture Jesus leaving Jewish territory, he usually spread the news of the God of Israel, inviting Gentiles into the realm.

Jesus *dressed* in a Jewish manner. The gospels report that he wore "fringes" (Mark 6:56; Matt. 9:20; Luke 8:44). Jewish people made fringes on the corners of their garments as a reminder to live according to the Commandments (Num. 15:37–40; Deut. 22:12). The wearing of the fringe was a sign of the intent to live in covenantal faithfulness. Some Jewish people continue this practice by wearing fringes on a prayer shawl or other special garments. Fringes today have the same meaning as in antiquity.

Jesus *observed the Sabbath*. The Sabbath (from sundown Friday to sundown Saturday) is the day God ordained for rest (Gen. 2:1–3; Exod. 20:8–11) and the day God later appointed for remembering that God delivered Israel from slavery (Deut. 5:12–15). While resting on the seventh day (Saturday) is a gift of God important in its own right, in the first century CE Sabbath observance became even more important as a symbol of ordering one's life according to Jewish values. Given the pressures of hellenization (see chap. 2), Sabbath observance was a means of maintaining Jewish identity. The Gospels repeatedly picture Jesus as observing the Sabbath in a Jewish manner (e.g., Mark 1:21; 6:2; Luke 4:16; 13:10). The Gospels also mention the disciples observing the Sabbath. Indeed, in a moving line, Luke says that after Jesus died, "On the sabbath they rested according to the commandment" (Luke 23:56).

Christians today sometimes accuse Jewish people in the first century of having legalistic attitudes about the Sabbath and of endlessly debating how much work one could do on it. This way of thinking is a Christian caricature. Jewish literature from the time is permeated by the recognition of the joy of the Sabbath. Christians sometimes think that Jesus debunked Sabbath practice. However, I will make the case that such reports were created by later communities to justify later church practices.

Jesus *participated in the synagogue* in the customary manner of the time. Synagogues, probably created during the Babylonian exile, were houses for worship, study, and community life. The Gospels consistently picture Jesus in the synagogue for worship. Local synagogue leaders often invited visiting rabbis (the word *rabbi* means "teacher") to speak. The Gospels frequently mention Jesus teaching in synagogues, presumably by such invitations, which indicates that other Jewish leaders respected him (e.g., Matt. 12:9; 26:55; Mark 1:21; 3:1; 6:2; Luke 4:15, 6:6; 13:10). Some scholars think of Matthew's congregation as a synagogue of the Jesus movement, that is, a synagogue that believed that Jesus was God's agent for manifesting the realm.

Jesus *prayed in a Jewish fashion.* The Gospels frequently refer to Jesus at prayer (e.g., Matt. 5:44; 14:23; 19:13; Mark 1:35; 6:46; Luke 3:21; 5:16; 6:12; 9:18, 28; 11:1). At a crucial moment of his life, with the cross ahead, the Gospels have Jesus praying (Matt. 26:36; Mark 14:32; Luke 22:41). Jesus taught the disciples to pray (Matt. 5:44; 6:5–8; 24:20; 26:41; Mark 11:25; 13:18; 14:38; Luke 11:2; 18:1; 22:40–46). Jesus' fullest instruction on prayer (the Lord's Prayer) includes a petition for the realm to come (Matt. 6:9–13; Luke 11:2–4). Christians today are so accustomed to offering this prayer in Christian worship that we seldom realize it is a *Jewish* prayer. From the Jewish address of God as "Father" through each petition, each element is drawn from Jewish ideas commonplace in the first century. Indeed, the prayer contains nothing distinctively Christian.

Jesus *dialogued in characteristic Jewish fashion with other Jewish people about how to be faithful.* Judaism in the first century CE was pluralistic. Different Jewish groups and leaders often discussed and even debated how best to interpret Torah and how to live conscientiously. Jesus' perspective was that the apocalypse is near. The Gospels recount Jesus' entering into such discussion about the coming of the realm and how to live in response to Torah in the way that many other Jewish people would have (e.g., Matt. 19:1–12; 21:23–27; 22:15–46; Mark 10:1–12, 17–31; 11:27–33; 12:13–37a; Luke 10:25–36; 20:1–8, 20–26, 27–44).

Contemporary Christians often mistakenly think Jesus rejected Judaism. However, many of Jesus' encounters with other Jewish people are typical of Jewish interactions in the first century, as we see by comparing them with discussions in the Talmud.[1] This situation is parallel to today's Christians disagreeing on whether abortion is acceptable. Moreover today's best biblical scholars conclude that the Gospel writers overemphasized the conflicts between Jesus and other Jewish people.

Jesus was *buried* following Jewish burial practices. His followers placed him in the tomb before sundown on Friday, and they planned to return to prepare his body by anointing him with spices for long-term entombment.

In the next chapter, I observe that that *Jesus commended following Torah* as a faithful way of life. I will also lift up a number of themes in his *teaching* that are characteristically Jewish.

How Was Jesus Different from Other First-Century Jewish People?

Jesus was at home in Judaism in the world of the first century. Indeed, he was an exponent of the Jewish vision of God and life. How, then, was he different from other Jewish people of the time? As this book has anticipated, the answer is that he expected the final manifestation of the realm of God to take place soon. His earliest followers, who were also Jewish, believed that the ministry of Jesus was itself not only a sign of that realm but a partial embodiment of it.

Jesus Portrayed as Having Conflict
with Other Jewish Leaders

If Jesus was such a faithful Jew, then why do the Gospels contain so many stories of Jesus in conflict with other Jewish leaders, notably the Pharisees, but also including scribes, Sadducees, lawyers, Herodians, and even some priests? As noted above, in part some such stories may stem from memories of Jesus in dialogue with other Jewish leaders regarding how to make theological sense of Jewish tradition.

However, another factor is involved in interpreting most of the stories of conflict between Jesus and Jewish leaders. In the decades after the fall of Jerusalem in 70 CE, tensions developed between the followers of Jesus and some Jewish people who did not believe that God was working through Jesus to finalize the realm. Because many of the followers of Jesus were Jewish, these tensions were really between two Jewish sects (and not between two distinct religions, Judaism and Christianity).[2]

The Gospel writers' communities, under the influence of the apocalyptic expectation, were incorporating Gentiles without asking the Gentiles to convert fully to Judaism. To be Gentile-friendly, the later communities invited Gentiles to repent and to turn to the God of Israel in preparation for the realm, but did not ask Gentiles to follow Jewish dietary practice or observe the Sabbath or to be circumcised.

After 70 CE, some Jewish communities thought that these actions by Jesus' followers compromised Judaism. Mark, Matthew, and Luke retrojected conflicts between the traditional synagogues and the communities of followers of Jesus back into the stories of Jesus and the leaders. The Gospel writers, then, do not recount occasions when the historical Jesus was face to face with historical Pharisees (and other Jewish leaders) of Jesus' own day, but rather the authors use the characters in the stories to speak to the situation of the later church. The Gospel writers use caricatures of the Pharisees in the stories to represent the Pharisees of their post-70 world. The Gospel writers use the character of Jesus in the story to speak a word that justifies the practices of Jesus' followers.

Examples: Plucking Grain and Healing
a Withered Hand on the Sabbath

The conflicts between Jesus and the Pharisees over plucking heads of grain on the Sabbath and over the healing of a person with a withered hand, as presented in Mark, are easy-to-follow examples of this phenomenon (Mark 2:23–3:6; cf. Matt. 12:1–14; Luke 6:1–11). In those days, roadways were often little more than paths. Jesus and his disciples were pictured as walking along a path that wound through a grain field, and when they became hungry, plucking some grain to eat. The Pharisees, who were also on the path, complained that Jesus and his disciples were violating Torah by working (plucking the grain). Jewish people in the first century would have known that typical Jewish interpretation of Torah permitted feeding hungry people on the Sabbath. However, Mark caricatures the Pharisees in order to persuade the community that Pharisees are untrustworthy, even corrupt.

Mark pictures Jesus replying in three parts. (1) Jesus cites 1 Samuel 21:1–6, where David is described as taking the bread of the Presence (sacred bread from the place of worship) in order to feed hungry companions. (2) Mark interprets the Sabbath as made for the needs of humankind, and not humankind for the Sabbath. (3) Mark makes the dramatic claim that the Son of Man (Jesus) is lord of the Sabbath. Mark uses Jesus' reply to justify the Markan church for its policy of not requiring Gentiles to observe the Sabbath.

A similar incident immediately follows (Mark 3:1–6). A person with a withered hand entered a synagogue where Jesus was present and the Pharisees were lurking to see whether Jesus would cure on the Sabbath "so that they might accuse him." Jesus invited the person with the withered hand to be healed and asked the Pharisees whether it is lawful to do good or to do harm on the Sabbath, but they were silent. The listeners knew that Jewish interpretation of Torah in the first century permitted actions to save life on the Sabbath. Mark even associated the Pharisees with Pharaoh by saying they have "hardness of heart."

After Jesus restored the hand, Marks says, "The Pharisees went out and immediately conspired with the Herodians against him, how to destroy him" (Mark 3:6). Mark portrays the Pharisees as vastly overreacting to the healing in the synagogue when they sought to kill

Jesus. Mark thereby discredits the Pharisees of Mark's own day and implies that they are untrustworthy, whereas Mark represents Jesus as ruler of the Sabbath. This latter affirmation was intended to empower Mark's church.

Examples of other stories that function similarly include: the healing of the paralytic (Mark 2:1–12; Matt. 9:1–8; Luke 5:17–26), the question about why Jesus and his disciples do not fast (Mark 2:18–22; Matt. 9:14–17; Luke 5:33–39), the charge that Jesus has a demon (Mark 3:21–22; Matt. 12:22–24; Luke 11:14–23), the questions about washing hands and eating unclean foods (Mark 7:1–23; Matt. 15:1–20), the woman who anointed Jesus with expensive perfume (Mark 14:3–9; Matt. 26:6–13; Luke 7:36–50), the long discourse against the Pharisees (Matt. 23:1–36; Luke 11:37–11:52), the healing of a bent-over woman (Luke 13:10–17), and the healing of a person with dropsy (Luke 14:1–6).

Here are two important observations. For one, Christians sometimes think that Jesus or the Gospel writers condemned Judaism as a whole. However a careful reading of the Gospels (including John) reveals that Jesus is never pictured as rejecting all Jewish people or Judaism itself. The Gospel writers carefully picture Jesus in tension with a few Jewish leaders. Even the crowds who turn against Jesus at the time of the crucifixion do not represent the whole Jewish population.

The other important observation is that a growing number of scholars think that the early church believed that the risen Jesus continued to communicate with them in order to fill out his teaching for their changing times.[3] Thus, the Gospel writers and their communities would not have regarded retrojecting their issues into the stories of Jesus as dishonest. They would have regarded it as theological interpretation in response to the continuing leading of Jesus.

Renouncing Anti-Judaism Today

A good many scholars today note that tensions between the communities of the Gospel writers and other Jewish communities did not constitute anti-Judaism since Jewish people in the churches were in tension with Jewish people in traditional synagogues. Indeed, Judaism was known for its prophetic self-criticism. However, while the caricatures in the Gospels are not anti-Judaism in the strict sense, they do go beyond prophetic self-criticism to misrepresentation for the purpose of justifying the church's attitudes and practices.

The caricatures of Jewish leaders that we find in all four Gospels are problematic in three ways. First, they are historically inaccurate. They leave the false impression that the Pharisees and other religious leaders were legalistic, viewed religion as based on works righteousness, and were hyper-combative. From the perspective of the Ten Commandments, such analysis amounts to the church bearing false witness against a neighbor. Second, the caricatures in the Gospels are bad theology because they imply that God does not love the Pharisees and other Jewish authorities. However, a God of unconditional love, by nature, loves the Pharisees as a part of loving each and all. Third, the misrepresentations of the Jewish leaders in the Gospels contribute to anti-Judaism and to the more virulent anti-Semitism. Such attitudes fueled the Holocaust, in which six million Jewish people were systematically murdered in Nazi Germany. Keeping these caricatures alive also helps keep anti-Semitism alive.

While we today might understand why the ancient Gospel writers and their communities developed such false impressions of Jewish leaders, the church is called to renounce these false ideas. The church is to tell the truth, and the truth is that we have lied in the ways we have painted many Jewish leaders from the world of the Bible (and many Jewish people since that time). The church does not need to justify our interpretation of the gospel and our practices by making Jewish people look bad. A growing Jewish-Christian dialogue over the past forty years suggests that the time is ripe for the church to explore how we might develop a mutual mission *with* Judaism to witness to God's love and God's will for justice for all.[4]

Questions for Discussion

1. Before reading this book, how had you imagined Jesus' relationship with Judaism? How does the picture of Jesus sketched in this chapter compare with your earlier thinking? What advantages do you see in the picture sketched in this book?

2. Think back over your life in the church. How have the Jewish people been portrayed in preaching and teaching? How does that picture compare with the ways in which the Jewish people are portrayed in this chapter?
3. If you had been a Gospel writer, how might you have tried to convey the church's openness to Gentiles without resorting to caricatures about Jewish leaders and Pharisees?
4. Does the church today misrepresent others in ways that remind you of the Gospel writers' misrepresentations of Judaism?

In the Questions for Discussion at the end of chapter 6, I suggest that you visit a synagogue and explore key aspects of Jewish identity with people there.

6

Realm Themes at the Center of the Teaching of Jesus

*C*hristians sometimes divide the ministry of Jesus into three parts—preaching, teaching, and actions. While this division cannot be pressed too far, it helps readers today understand different moments in Jesus' ministry. The preaching of Jesus announces that the realm of God is partially present and is about to come to final and full manifestation, and Jesus invites people to prepare by repentance. The teaching of Jesus explains the realm and helps people live according to its values. The actions of Jesus demonstrate the realm by putting it into action.

The necessary brevity of this chapter means that we can only highlight how the realm of God permeates the teaching of Jesus. After beginning with the Jewish character of the teaching of Jesus, we turn to the realm as a key to the teaching of Jesus, and to the Great Commandment, which is central in the teaching of Jesus. The chapter then focuses on the teaching of Jesus as helping people embody the realm in everyday life and on the parables as preparation for the realm. We conclude by reflecting on Jesus' wariness toward Rome and on the teaching of Jesus in today's world.

The Jewish Teaching of Jesus

Christians sometimes see the teaching of Jesus as contrasting with the teaching of Judaism. Christians occasionally speak of the teaching of Jesus as calling people to a higher righteousness than that of Judaism. Indeed, some Christians see Jesus' instructions as altogether new in their radicality. These perspectives are mistaken.

Scholars today stress that the teaching of Jesus is essentially Jewish. As we pointed out in the previous chapter, Jewish teachers in the first century CE had different interpretations of Jewish tradition, and Jesus' teaching is part of this ongoing dialogue in Judaism. Even the seemingly radical elements of Jesus' teaching were not new, but applied core Jewish convictions to the first century CE. As a teacher, Jesus stands in the prophetic tradition adapted by the apocalyptic perspective (see chap. 3). Where the teaching of Jesus differed most from other Jewish pedagogues of the same period was with regard to the timetable for the realm.

The Realm of God as Key to the Teaching of Jesus

We do not have space to focus on many details in the teaching of Jesus. However, the realm of God is a key by which you can make sense of almost any specific instruction from Jesus. From the perspective of the realm, Jesus' teaching has three loci. (1) Jesus seeks to help people recognize that the brokenness of the present age is not what God wants. (2) Jesus seeks to help people avoid complicity with the forces and behaviors of the present evil age, and especially to avoid the consequences—both in the present and in the future—of living by old-age values. (3) Jesus encourages his followers to live in the present (as much as possible), as if the realm is already present here—a particular emphasis in the Gospels.

Jesus' teaching thus guides people away from alliance with Satan and the demons, from idolatry and fractiousness, from assuming that injustice, poverty, and sickness are to be expected, and from violence and death. Jesus' teaching points listeners toward God, restored relationships, and community in which people live together much as they did in Eden. Indeed, when the realm is fully instantiated, violence and death will be replaced by peace and eternal life.

The Great Commandment: Guide to Life

No single passage completely sums up the teaching of Jesus. However, the text that comes closest is the giving of the Great Commandment (Mark 12:28–34; Matt. 22:34–40; Luke 10:25–37). In Mark and Matthew, someone asks Jesus which commandment is the first of all.

This question was already being discussed among Jewish leaders of Jesus' time. Jesus' answer thus does not introduce a new issue in the Jewish world but locates Jesus and the disciples in that first-century discussion.

The query about which commandment is first is a question about what beliefs are central to Jewish identity and that of Jesus' followers. Jesus put together two texts from Jewish tradition. Mark has Jesus cite Deuteronomy 6:4 as follows: "Hear, O Israel: the Lord our God, the Lord is one; you shall love the Lord your God with all your heart, and with all your soul, and with all your mind, and with all your strength." Leviticus 19:18 says, "You shall love your neighbor as yourself."

By putting these two texts together, Jesus and the Gospel writers assert that for both traditional Jews and members of Jesus' realm movement, identity is defined by loving God and neighbor. Matthew notes, "On these two commandments hang all the law and the prophets" (Matt. 22:40). Matthew's Jesus sees Torah as helping the community know how to love both God and neighbor. Other Jewish thinkers from Jesus' day offered similar formulations.[1] For example, the apocalyptic *Testament of Dan* says, "Throughout all your life, love the Lord and one another with a true heart" (5:3).[2]

By the time of Mark, Matthew, and Luke, the temple had been destroyed, thus making it impossible to engage in sacrificial rites. Mark is quite explicit in this regard by pointing out that this commandment is "much more important than all whole burnt offerings and sacrifices" (Mark 12:33). The point is that one can be Jewish without a temple by following the Great Commandment. One can follow Jewish tradition without a temple but not without the core of Torah.

The communities of Mark, Matthew, and Luke welcomed Gentiles. Jesus' interpretation of the Great Commandment makes it possible for Gentiles to body forth an essential aspect of the faithful Jewish life (loving God and neighbor) while awaiting the apocalypse. Torah can thus guide Gentiles in living toward the realm.

Embody the Realm in Everyday Life

Much of the teaching of Jesus guides the community in embodying the realm in everyday life. The community does not rely solely on its own will in order to follow Jesus' teaching. The immediacy of the realm means that possibilities for perception and behavior are no longer limited by the strictures of the present evil age. The realm creates a force field within which people are empowered to follow the teaching of Jesus.

For illustration, I turn to the Sermon on the Mount (Matt. 5:1–7:27; cf. Luke 6:17–49).[3] It begins with the Beatitudes, which, for Matthew, are not commands but are assurances to particular groups of people that they will be blessed by being included in the realm (Matt. 5:1–12). For example, "those who mourn" refers not to people who are sad simply because death has visited their immediate worlds but to those who mourn the brokenness of the old age. They know that God intends blessing for all, so they mourn the fact that so many live such fractured, impoverished, violent lives. Those who mourn in this way will be comforted, that is, welcomed into the realm (Matt. 5:4).

After reminding listeners that Torah is their guide as they await the realm (5:17–20), Matthew illustrates the interpretation of Torah in view of the immediate coming of the realm (5:21–48). These sayings follow the same pattern: a recollection that "You have heard it said" (in a passage from the First Testament), "but I [Jesus] say to you." These statements are sometimes called the "antitheses," as if the teaching of Jesus is antithetical to Jewish tradition. A better way of understanding these statements is to see them as extending the implication of the First Testament as it is empowered by possibilities for behavior created as the realm becomes present.

According to Matthew 6:1–18 and 7:1–12, the disciples are to engage in prayer, almsgiving, and other spiritual practices according to the highest Jewish standards. In the previous chapter I mentioned that the Prayer for the Realm (the Lord's Prayer, Matt. 6:9–13) is Jewish in content. Matthew draws from deep wells of Jewish confidence in the providence of God in 6:19–34 to assure people that God can care for them during the difficult times that precede the apocalypse.

The Sermon on the Mount closes with a reminder of one of the most important Jewish values. The community is to bear good fruit by doing the will of God. They are to live the values of the realm urged by Torah, interpreted apocalyptically (Matt. 7:13–27). Matthew has four other large concentrations of Jesus' teaching, each with its own theme: 10:5–42 (mission); 13:1–52 (parables of the realm); 18:1–35 (discipline and forgiveness in community); and 24:3–25:46 (preparation for the end of the world).

Mark, Matthew, and Luke often embed the teaching of Jesus in responses to questions from Jesus' followers or in accounts of conflicts between Jesus and Jewish authorities. In Mark the longest direct teaching discourses motivate the disciples to remember that the apocalypse is ahead (Mark 4:1–34) and provide practical instruction in interpreting events of Mark's day as signs of the coming apocalypse (Mark 13:1–37). Mark also presents bits and pieces of teaching in shorter passages. For example, when James and John request seats on Jesus' right and left hands in the realm, Mark stresses that Jesus' followers are not to seek power according to the standards of the old age but are to serve the values of the realm (Mark 10:35–45).

The paradigmatic instance of Jesus' teaching in Luke is Jesus' sermon at Nazareth when Jesus interprets his ministry as pointing toward the year of God's favor (the realm) (Luke 4:16–22) and as ultimately leading to the Gentile mission (4:23–30).With respect to the timetable of the realm, Luke prepares the community for a delay. This development is particularly clear in the book of Acts, where Jesus' followers organize patterns for providing for the poor and the church elects deacons to care for widows over a long period (Acts 2:41–48; 4:32–35; 6:1–6).

The Parables: Prepare for the Realm

The parables found in Mark, Matthew, and Luke (but not in John) are among the most memorable of Jesus' methods of teaching. Parables often work by inviting listeners to identify positively with the beginning of the story, but bringing listeners up short by an unexpected development and prompting them to reflect on their perception and behavior.

Some interpreters like to speak of the shocking character of the parables. However, we should not think all the parables have a single function or all work in the same way. Some parables end on a provocative note that leaves listeners contemplating what to make of it. Other parables contain a statement of direct application to listeners. Some parables are illustrations. By using parables, Jesus took up a teaching method used by other Jewish teachers.

The distinctive quality of the parables is that they focus on the realm.[4] Indeed, many of the parables explicitly begin "The realm of God is like . . ." Some parables that do not explicitly contain that introductory formula still have the realm as their subject matter. The parables of the realm seek to encourage listeners to reflect on things such as the adequacy of their understanding of the realm of God or on their preparedness for it. As is the case with other aspects of the teaching of Jesus, the Gospel writers have so woven the parables into their particular Gospel narratives that it is very difficult to identify what Jesus may actually have said or how particular parables functioned before being written into the Gospels. Nevertheless, we can often describe how the Gospel writers use the parables, and many scholars think that the emphasis on the realm goes back to Jesus himself.

As an example, we see these themes in the parable of the Mustard Seed in Mark 4:30–32 (cf. Matt. 13:31–32; Luke 13:18–19): "With what can we compare the [realm] of God, or what parable will we use for it? It is like a mustard seed, which, when sown upon the ground, is the smallest of all the seeds on earth; yet when it is sown it grows up and becomes the greatest of all shrubs, and puts forth large branches, so that the birds of the air can make nests in its shade." This parable compares the final manifestation of the realm of God to the contrast between the tiny mustard seed and the bush that grows from it.

The community to which Mark wrote after the fall of the temple in 70 CE was discouraged and losing hope that the realm would come. In Mark's view, the ministry of Jesus and the witness of the community are like the mustard seed: almost invisible. Yet, when the apocalypse comes, the realm will contrast with the old age as the mustard seed contrasts with the bush. Furthermore, Jewish literature in antiquity sometimes portrays Gentiles as birds (e.g., Ezek. 17:23; 31:5–6; Dan. 4:12; *1 En.* 90:2–3, 30–37; *Jos. Asen.* 15:7). The parable thus challenges the community's discouragement and urges community members to remember that the realm will include Gentiles.

Be Wary of the State

The opposition of Jesus to Rome is one of the most popular themes in scholarship on Jesus in the early twenty-first century. Indeed, occasional contemporary writers think that Jesus' primary focus was criticizing Rome and that Jesus sought to organize a resistance movement that would transform the Roman Empire. Most scholars agree that Jesus and his followers did sharply criticize Rome. However, I agree with the scholars who think such singular focus on Rome is reductionism and that Jesus was concerned with the full range of brokenness in the old age. Furthermore, the apocalyptic interpretation of Jesus and the Gospels in this book suggests that Jesus believed God would end Roman rule and not that Jesus intended to promote resistance that would lead to the transformation of the empire. The witness of Jesus (and the Gospels) against Rome is a prophetic warning to the disciples (and the congregations of Mark, Matthew, and Luke) not to seek security in Rome but to repent of collusion with the empire and to wait patiently for the realm.

Jesus seldom spoke directly about Rome. However, the apocalyptic worldview is itself the most trenchant criticism of Rome. For the apocalyptic theologians believed that Rome would be destroyed with the old age and that the realm would become the means by which the new world is governed.

Jesus' most direct statement about Rome comes in response to the question of whether one should pay taxes to the emperor. "Give to the emperor the things that are the emperor's, and to God the things that are God's" (Mark 12:17; cf. Matt. 22:15–22; Luke 20:20–26). Christians typically think that Jesus' reply means that people should respect both the civil government (by paying taxes) and also religious institutions (by putting money in the offering plate). However, the question that Jesus asks, "Whose head is this [on the coin]?" is better translated "Whose image is this?" Since the image on the coin was that of a human being, and human beings are made in the image of God, a faithful Jew would recognize the image as the image of God and would know that (a) a human being is to serve God's purpose of helping all experience blessing, and that (b) the empire worked against this purpose. Indeed, some emperors minted coins depicting themselves in close association with the gods, thus moving toward idolatry. Jesus' response subtly implies that the emperor is idolatrous and that the empire has no lasting authority.

The Gospel writers directly criticize Rome by naming the Gerasene demoniac as Legion. The word *legion* referred to a Roman military unit. By making this association, the Gospel writers suggest that Rome itself is possessed (Mark 5:1–20; Matt. 8:28–34; Luke 8:26–39). The Gospel writers are also stressing that Pilate, the Roman governor, made the decision to put Jesus to death (Mark 15:6–15; Matt. 27:15–26; Luke 23:17–25). Crucifixion was a distinctively Roman form of capital punishment.

Jesus and the Gospel writers also criticize Rome by criticizing the officials who ruled the eastern Mediterranean in behalf of Rome. Mark uses the story of Herod ordering the beheading of John the Baptist to warn the community to expect Herod-like behavior from civil officials in the last days (Mark 6:17–29; cf. 8:15). Matthew expands on such warnings (Matt. 2:13–23; 14:3–12). Luke implicates Herod in the death of Jesus (Luke 23:6–16). The writers thus warn listeners to be wary of the state. When a government begins to act like Rome or its puppet, Herod, the community is called to witness to the ways such governments violate God's purposes.

The Teaching of Jesus Today

Jesus intended his teaching as a guide for people in the short interim between Jesus' moment in history and the apocalypse, and not for people two thousand years later. Jesus spoke to people who lived in the first century CE under very different conditions than we live in today. The apocalypse has not occurred. The Roman Empire no longer rules, and many other aspects of our situation differ from the life presupposed by Jesus and the Gospel writers.

Some of Jesus' teaching can be directly instructive today. For example, Jesus says, "Love your enemies, do good to those who hate you, bless those who curse you, pray for those who abuse you" (Luke 6:27–28). While we may need to explore what Jesus meant by loving your enemies and the other items in this list, the plain force of the teaching is clear. But some of Jesus' teaching hardly makes sense if we try to apply it directly. Who in the church today, for instance, is concerned with congregants sounding a trumpet before they give alms (Matt. 6:1–4)?

Much of the teaching of Jesus can be very helpful if we take it not as direct instruction for us but approach it by way of analogy. In reference to particular teachings, Christians can ask, What circumstances and experiences function similarly in our culture as those presumed by the specific teaching? How might Jesus' guidance in that situation function similarly today? For example, while few in the church today are concerned about sounding a trumpet before almsgiving, we might ask, Who in our setting engages in beneficial public works but in a way that shifts the focus from the need for which the gift is intended to the public recognition and power of the giver? (see Matt. 6:1–4).

Occasionally, of course, the church may need to consider whether a particular teaching of Jesus is really consistent with our deepest convictions about God's purposes for the world. This is especially likely in the case of texts that caricature Jewish people, as described in the previous chapter.

Questions for Discussion

1. Before reading this chapter, what would you have said were the main themes of the teaching of Jesus? What would you say now?

2. Do the economic networks created by transnational corporations (centered in the United States and Europe) function in our world in ways that are similar to the function of the Roman Empire in antiquity? Are recent attitudes and actions of the U.S. government both abroad and at home similar to Roman imperialism? How might you criticize these efforts from the perspective of the realm of God?

3. Using the principle of analogy, consider how you might interpret Jesus' teaching to the Twelve to travel lightly when Jesus sent them into mission (Luke 9:1–6).

Judaism has evolved since the first century. However, core aspects of Jewish identity have continued. If possible, make arrangements to worship with a synagogue and to meet with some synagogue members afterward. Keeping chapters 5 and 6 in mind, note where you see aspects of Jewish life and teaching that would have been familiar to Jesus. Perhaps the people with whom you meet afterward would offer their interpretations of the core of Jewish identity and mission.

Jesus Demonstrates the Realm through Miracles

A question that puzzles a good many people today is whether Jesus actually performed miracles. That question was not central for people in antiquity. As far as we can tell, they generally believed that miracles happened. For ancient communities, the primary issue was the meaning of miracles. How should a miracle be interpreted? What should a community learn from a miraculous occurrence? Not surprisingly, for the Gospel writers, the miracles of Jesus embody the presence of the realm of God.

As a way of getting acclimated to how first-century people viewed miracle stories, we will first look at some examples of miracle workers in antiquity. We will meditate on the miracles of Jesus as demonstrations of the realm of God. We will consider four kinds of miracles—healings of the sick, exorcisms, nature miracles, and occasions when a miracle is a platform for Jesus (or the Gospel writer) to make a point. We conclude by asking, What about miracles for today?

The Gospel of John also contains stories of miraculous events. John, however, refers to these miracles as signs, and their function is different from that of the miracle stories in Mark, Matthew, and Luke. We consider the signs in chapter 10.

I discourage Christians today from referring to miracles as supernatural events. People in antiquity did not use the term *supernatural*. They did not divide the world into natural and supernatural arenas. They did not have a concept of natural law. For them, the world was a single theater of divine activity in which deities could be active in different ways. A miracle was not a supernatural violation of natural law but an occasion when God acted to make a particular point.

Miracle Working in Antiquity

Miracles were not reported to take place on every street corner every day in antiquity, but people in antiquity were familiar enough with miraculous events that their focus was on the connotations of the miracles more than on the events themselves.[1] Miracle stories could express compassion for people in dire situations, prove the trustworthiness of the deity, reinforce the authority of the miracle worker, show that an idea is true, become an occasion to teach a lesson, or represent important values.

The First Testament contains stories of miracles. For example, through Elijah God provided for the widow of Zarephath (1 Kgs. 17:8–16) and resuscitated the widow's child (1 Kgs. 17:17–24). Through Elisha, God fed one hundred people with barley (2 Kgs. 4:42–44) and cured Naaman of leprosy (2 Kgs. 5:1–19). Such stories name God as the miracle-working power and establish the authority of the prophets while exhibiting divine concern for wholeness of life.

About the time of Jesus, Judaism contained a number of miracle workers. During drought, for instance, Honi the Circle Drawer prayed for rain. When nothing happened, he drew a circle and refused to leave it until God had mercy on the community by giving rain.[2] Hanina ben Dosa was a healer. A child of a well-known rabbi became sick, and two people went to Hanina and asked the healer to come to the house where the child was. Instead, Hanina went to "his upper room and prayed for mercy" for the child. When the visitors returned home, they found the child cured.[3] Rabbi Gamaliel was on a ship that was about to be swamped by a giant wave in a storm. The rabbi prayed and the sea subsided.[4] These stories demonstrate the mercy of God and are designed to inspire the community to respect the authority of not only the miracle workers but the Talmud, in which their stories were told.

The Miracles of Jesus Demonstrate the Realm of God

The Gospels present the miracles of Jesus as functioning like other miracles in the ancient world.[5] Additionally, the most important function of the miracles of Jesus is to demonstrate the realm of God. The miracles show that the realm is already becoming manifest through the ministry of Jesus, and they also embody the purposes of the realm (e.g., Matt. 11:2–6; 12:15–21; Luke 4:16–19; 7:18–28). Indeed, the miracles are almost mini-apocalypses in the sense that God through Jesus confronts a power (e.g., sickness, demon, element of nature) that distorts God's purposes for human life and corrects that distortion. The diminished person or situation is restored in much the same way that apocalyptic thinkers anticipated restoration in the realm of God.

Not only does the person or community involved in the miracle experience the momentary realization of the realm through the miracle, but later communities who hear the miracle *stories* have a similar experience through their imaginations. Hearers identify with the characters in the story and experience the unfolding of the plot. To be sure, the recipients of the miracles were restored for continued life in the old age and they would eventually die. However, the miracles strengthen the hope for the new world for the recipients and for those who heard their stories.

When turning to specific miracle stories, it is important to remember that the Gospel writers interpret these stories. In the remarks that follow I often call attention to how the Gospel writers use these stories. I discuss the miracle stories in three categories used by many scholars—nature miracles, exorcisms, healings. Scholars also refer to a fourth category—raisings from the dead—but I take up this category in chapter 9.

We can hear many of the miracle stories from two (sometimes related) perspectives. Of course the stories refer to people and events. Beyond that—especially meaningful to many Christians today and as we see in the studies that follow—many elements evoke themes from the First Testament to represent broader aspects of experience.

Nature Miracles

The nature miracles begin with a person or group in a situation of threat caused by some aspect of nature. Through the miracle, God removes the threat and returns the situation to God's purposes of love, peace, security, and abundance. Matthew's story of Jesus walking on the water is such a miracle (Matt. 14:22–33). As just noted, the Gospel writer has shaped this story to communicate a particular message to his own congregation. Matthew uses the figure of Jesus to represent the risen Jesus.

Jesus was praying alone on a mountain while the disciples got in a boat. Scholars note that in the case of a previous incident involving a storm on the sea (Matt. 8:23–27), Matthew used the word "followed" (a technical term for discipleship) to associate the boat with the community of Jesus' followers.[6] The reader thus assumes that the boat in the story of Jesus walking on the water also represents the community of disciples.

The boat was battered by waves and wind. Before God began to form the world as it now is, the cosmos was a vast, wild, stormy, unfocused chaos (Gen. 1:1–2). Consequently, in Jewish literature in antiquity, the sea often represents chaos. The disciples in the boat thus bespeak Matthew's perception that the community to which he wrote the Gospel was in chaos (e.g., Matt. 5:10–12; 5:43–48; 10:17–33; 13:21; 24:4–25).

Jesus walked on the water to the boat. When the disciples failed to recognize Jesus, he spoke a word of assurance to them. "Take heart, it is I; do not be afraid." By describing Jesus coming to them on the water, the writer assured the community that Jesus would come to them even in the midst of chaos.

Jesus invited Peter to walk to Jesus on the water. Peter left the boat and started walking toward Jesus but became frightened, began to sink, and called out, "[Jesus], save me." Immediately Jesus caught Peter by the hand, and said, "You of little faith, why did you doubt?" Matthew often characterizes the disciples as people of "little faith," that is, followers who are still maturing in discipleship (Matt. 6:30; 8:26; 16:8; 17:20).

Peter's situation in the boat is like that of the Matthean community. Jesus calls them to leave the security of the boat and step into mission, with particular focus on bringing Gentiles into the community (Matt. 28:16–20), as well as to embody the realm in the other ways that Jesus taught (e.g., 5:1–7:27; 10:5–42; 13:1–52; 18:1–35; 24:3–25:46). For Matthew, then, this miracle story assures the community that as they do what Jesus commanded, even in their chaotic situation, they can be assured that Jesus is with them and that Jesus will ultimately rescue them when the realm comes in its fullness.

Exorcising Demons

To recap a theme from chapter 2, the apocalyptic worldview held that Satan exercised great power in the present evil age and that the demons were Satan's agents. Many ancient Jewish people believed that the demons were personal spirits who would inhabit individuals or communities and direct them to serve Satan.

The day after Jesus and the disciples had seen Jesus transfigured, they encountered a parent with a child possessed by a demon (Luke 9:37–43). The demon would seize the child and cause the child to shriek and convulse and to foam at the mouth. Indeed, the demon would maul the child. The situation of the child was similar to the situation of the world in the old age: just as the demons were destroying the life of the child, so they were fracturing the life of the world.

However, Jesus rebuked the unclean spirit (another name for demons) and returned the child to the parent. Luke's message is clear: in the presence of Jesus, the demons lose their power, and qualities of the realm prevail. Although the disciples could not cast out *this* demon, after they received the Holy Spirit on Pentecost (Acts 2:1–38), they, too, could enact exorcism as signs of the realm (Acts 5:12–16; 8:4–8; 19:11–20).

Few people today believe in demons as personal beings, but we do know forces that take controlling roles in individuals and groups, guiding them to do things they might not freely choose to do. Substance addiction, for instance, possesses individuals. At a social level, systemic racism is a demon that possesses culture in the United States. Even people of European origin who oppose racism benefit from the racism ingrained in our society and are implicated in racist patterns of behavior. Until our social world is reconstituted, the most a Eurocentric person can hope to be is a racist who is anti-racist.

Healing the Sick

Nearly every time I teach the miracle stories, I confront a misconception. Many contemporary Christians think that everyone in antiquity believed that sickness was the result of sin. While some ancient people did think that, not all did. Occasionally people influenced by apocalypticism thought that sickness resulted from demonic possession, but most thought illness was a manifestation of the brokenness of the present age. A healing, therefore, unveiled the presence and future of the realm.

Mark 8:22–26 tells of an encounter between Jesus and a blind person. Jesus used healing gestures typical of the time by placing saliva on his hands and touching the eyes of the blind person who, initially, could see people who were so indistinct that they looked like trees walking. Jesus laid hands on the blind person a second time, and the sight was restored.

Christians today are sometimes perplexed by the fact that Jesus did not heal the blind person with one gesture. However, such perplexity misses the way Mark uses this story. In Jewish literature, blindness refers both to a physical condition and to the inability to perceive. The two-stage healing represents what needs to happen to the disciples in Mark. At this point in the narrative, the disciples have received a first touch. Mark has presented Jesus as the agent of the realm but has only emphasized Jesus as miracle worker and teacher. The disciples are like the person in the narrative: they can see Jesus partially, because they see him only as a great miracle worker, and they expect the miraculous coming of the realm.

However, in order to understand Jesus more fully, the disciples need a second touch, that is, they need to understand that as a part of the final manifestation of the realm, Jesus will suffer, and they will suffer. They receive this second touch in Mark 8:27–9:1 and in subsequent events. The Markan community, like the disciples, needs this second touch in order to endure the suffering of the last days before the apocalypse.

Making Sense of the Miracles Today

Some people today try to rationalize what happened in the miracles by explaining them as ordinary occurrences. For example, I continue to hear people explain the walking-on-the-water story as follows: the boat was near the shore and Jesus was walking at the edge of the lake; in the dim light, the disciples did not realize they were close to shore and only thought Jesus was walking on the water. To explain the feedings of the thousands, contemporary folk sometimes say that some people in antiquity took picnic baskets into the wilderness and hid the baskets under their robes; when Jesus broke the loaves, the people got out their baskets and shared their food. The real miracle is thus the sharing.

These efforts are well intentioned in trying to help people today make sense of the miracle stories. However, the Bible itself gives these versions no support. People in antiquity believed that miraculous events took place. As I perceive the world today, such events do not take place routinely. Indeed, I think churches offer people an unreliable hope to suggest that people today can expect miracles of the kind reported in the Bible.[7]

Nevertheless, the miracle stories make an important point that is significant for many people today. Below the surface events of the miracles, a deeper point abides. These stories use first-century language and images to affirm that God is ever at work in each distorted situation in life to help restore that situation. Dramatic turnarounds, such as those reported in the miracle stories, are unusual in the early twenty-first century. Yet in many difficult situations we can sense a lure toward restoration or an experience of the presence of providence that moves in the direction of the realm.

Anne Wire, a scholar of the Second Testament, notices that the circumstances that call forth the miracle are like a circle or a mold. People feel that their possibilities for life are bounded, closed by the circle or diminished by the mold. The situation limits the capacity of the people in the situation to enter fully into life as God intends. The miracle story declares that we are not imprisoned, but that God is present and seeks to open the circle, or break open the mold.[8] However, even when a circumstance does not change, our perspective within the circumstance can change in liberating ways, especially as we perceive God with us as companion on the journey toward renewal.

Questions for Discussion

1. As you approach the subject of Jesus' miracles, what do you remember hearing about the miracles in the past? Have you thought of them as actual events? Have you rationalized them? How does the perspective of this chapter influence your thinking?
2. Many people in antiquity in addition to Jesus were reported to perform miracles. How might you incorporate that idea into your own perspective on Jesus?
3. Think of the nature miracles that evoke chaos through water or wilderness symbolism. Where do you identify the threat of chaos in the world today? Where do you feel that threat in your life? How do you experience a lure toward restoration? How can you respond to that lure and join God in trying to manifest qualities of the realm in that situation?
4. Thinking of exorcisms, where you do see individuals or communities today who are possessed by systemic deformations of life or other forms of possession? How do you experience a lure toward restoration? How can you respond to that lure and join God in trying to manifest qualities of the realm in that situation?

Rejecting the Realm: Crucifixion

Although specific language about the realm of God does not often appear in the narratives of the last week of the life of Jesus, the writers of the first three Gospels have set the stage for listeners to understand the events of this week as a struggle between the realm of God and rulers of the present evil age. The Gospel writers interpret Jesus as Messiah (Christ) and as God's agent for the final manifestation of the realm, and they underscore that this manifestation brings about the rejection and death of Jesus (e.g., Mark 8:27–33; Matt. 16:13–23; Luke 9:18–22).[1] The events of the last week of Jesus' life, especially the betrayal, trial, and crucifixion, are defining moments in the apocalyptic struggle between the realm of God and Satan and the powers of the old age.

In this chapter, we first consider how the Gospels portray the Jewish people, especially Jewish leaders, in the death of Jesus. We consider the entry into Jerusalem, the Last Supper, and the betrayal, arrest, trial, and crucifixion.

The Gospels Caricature the Responsibility of the Jewish Leaders

Christians sometimes say "the Jews killed Jesus" and even call Jewish people today "Christ-killers." Although these words do not fall from Christian lips as often as they once did, the attitudes that they communicate do still linger in some corners of the Christian house in the form of anti-Judaism and anti-Semitism. The Gospels, however, indicate that Rome (and not

Jewish officials) put Jesus to death. None of the Gospel writers hold the Jewish people as a whole accountable for the death of Jesus. Many scholars today think that the Gospel writers exaggerate the role of the Jewish leaders in the death of Jesus in order to justify the tension between the communities of Jesus' followers and traditional Jewish communities after the fall of Jerusalem in 70 CE (see chap. 4).

The Representative of the Realm Enters Jerusalem

For the first three Gospels, the arrival of Jesus in the Holy City is rightly called the entry into Jerusalem rather than Palm Sunday. Mark and Matthew have the crowd waving tree branches while Luke omits this detail. John alone directly mentions palm branches (Mark 11:1–10; Matt. 21:1–9; Luke 19:28–38; John 12:12–19).

The Gospel writers tell about Jesus entering Jerusalem in such a way as to recollect how ancient rulers often entered cities. By spreading their cloaks, the crowd acknowledged that Jesus was an important figure. Jesus arrived as representative of the realm. By riding on a donkey, Jesus indicated that he came in peace. The crowds in Mark and Matthew waved branches that remind listeners of the Maccabean revolt in 168–165 BCE, when the Maccabees family led a Jewish revolt against the occupying ruler, Antiochus IV Epiphanes. When the Jewish people entered the freed Jerusalem, they waved branches, which then became a symbol of liberation (1 Macc. 13:49–53).

The word *hosanna* was not a shout of praise (as Christians today often think); it means "save us." The crowd identifies Jesus with David as if Jesus was about to re-establish a Davidic style of national independence. Congregations today seldom realize that the crowds did not recognize Jesus in his role as representative of the apocalyptic realm.

The Last Supper as Realm Meal

All three Gospels regard the feedings of the thousands as the background for understanding the Last Supper. Many Jewish people influenced by apocalypticism believed that after the apocalypse and the uninhibited manifestation of the realm, God would host a vast celebratory meal (sometimes called the eschatological or messianic banquet).

The Gospel writers see the feedings of the multitudes as anticipating this event (Mark 6:30–44; 8:1–20; Matt. 14:13–21; 15:32–39; Luke 9:10–17).

Both the feedings and the Last Supper report that Jesus *took* bread, *blessed* it, *broke* it, and *gave* it. The Gospel writers regard the Last Supper as the institution of the sacred meal of the church with bread and cup. The use of the words *took*, *blessed*, *broke*, and *gave* indicates the writers understood the sacred meal as an anticipation of the final eschatological banquet. Just as this meal provided assurance for Jesus just before the crucifixion, so it assured the community of God's ultimate victory, even as community members lived through the difficult season of tribulation just before the apocalypse.

Churches have developed complicated theories to explain the sayings "This is my body" and "This is my blood of the covenant." I have already alluded to the best (and relatively simple) explanation. Jewish people in antiquity believed that essential qualities of past and future events could come to life in the present. The references to the body and blood of the covenant have to do, not with a metaphysical transformation of the bread and cup, but with the events of the crucifixion and resurrection as sealing the promise (or covenant) of the realm. When the community says, "This is my body . . . this is my blood," community members experience the risen Jesus and the realm as present during the sacred meal.

Betrayal, Arrest, and Denial

The Gospels negatively portray the roles of the disciples in the last week of Jesus' life. All three Gospels identify Judas as the betrayer of Jesus (Mark 14:10–11; Matt. 26:14–16; Luke 22:3–6). Matthew indicates that Judas's motive was greed, a characteristic of the old age. Thirty pieces of silver was a small amount of money, for example, the price of a slave who had been gored by an ox (Exod. 21:32). Matthew derived this detail from Zechariah 11:12–13 and 13:7–9, where it is associated with a worthless shepherd who intended to destroy the flock. Judas was such a shepherd and was condemned accordingly (Matt. 27:3–10). Luke says that Satan entered Judas. Luke, too, declares that Judas was judged (Acts 1:15–20).

After the Last Supper, Jesus prayed in Gethsemane, an olive orchard on the Mount of Olives across a valley east of the temple (Mark 14:32–42; Matt. 26:36–46; Luke 22:40–46). This detail recalls Zechariah 14:1–5, envisioning God on the Mount of Olives as a part of an apocalyptic transformation. Jesus, aware of his impending death, asked the disciples to keep awake while he prayed, but they failed him by sleeping.

According to the first three Gospels, a crowd with swords and clubs came to arrest Jesus (Mark 14:43–52; Matt. 26:47–56; Luke 22:47–53). The kiss by which Judas betrayed Jesus exposed the corruptness of the old age. A kiss was supposed to be a gesture of friendship, but Judas reversed its purpose. Jesus asked, "Have you come out with swords and clubs to arrest me as though I were a bandit?" The word *bandit* sounds to North Americans as if it refers to a thief, but in first-century culture it typically referred to someone involved in rebellion.[2] The crowd thus completely misperceived Jesus, who had no interest in fomenting political rebellion.

By reporting that the disciples behave in ways characteristic of the old age, the Gospel writers press listeners to ask whether they, too, continue to think and act from the perspective of the old age. Christians can still consider this issue today.

The Trial

While the Gospel writers share the same general outline of the trial(s) of Jesus, they differ on some details (Mark 14:53–15:15; Matt. 26:57–27:25; Luke 22:54–62). In describing the trial, Mark, Matthew, and Luke engage in some of their most flagrant caricatures of Jewish leaders. The Gospel writers also pass judgment on Pilate and Rome.

The mob takes Jesus to the council, the Sanhedrin, the ruling body of Judaism (Mark 14:53–72; Matt. 26:57–75; Luke 22:54–71). The Gospel writers portray the council as violating its own regulations.[3] (1) A trial should be held in the daytime, but Jesus was tried at night. (2) A trial should take place over two consecutive days, whereas Jesus' trial occurred in one night. (3) The Hall of Hewn Stones was to be the location of a trial, whereas the trial of Jesus took place at the home of the high priest. (4) Witnesses should be questioned privately, whereas at the trial of Jesus the witnesses not only testified publicly but were coached to give false testimony by Jewish leaders. (5) The reasons for acquittal should be given first, whereas at the trial of Jesus, false testimony concerning his guilt was the initial evidence. (6) The council should warn witnesses to testify accurately, whereas at this trial the leaders encouraged witnesses to give false testimony.

Mark and Matthew report that an important piece of evidence was the false statement that Jesus had declared he would destroy the temple and rebuild it in three days. No such statement can be found in the first two Gospels. Mark editorializes, "But even on this point their testimony did not agree." The high priest then asks, "Are you the Messiah?" In Mark Jesus answers straightforwardly ("I am"), whereas in Matthew and Luke his response is ambiguous. In all three Gospels, however, Jesus asserts that they will soon see the Son of Man (Jesus) returning from the right hand of God (in heaven). In other words, Jesus will return at the apocalypse.

The high priest then declared that Jesus committed blasphemy. In Judaism blasphemy consisted of reviling the name of God or of claiming for oneself qualities that were associated only with God. Jesus did not do either of these things. The Gospel writers picture the high priest as misunderstanding his own tradition.

When morning broke, the council delivered Jesus to Pilate, who alone had power to put people to death. Matthew and Mark depict Pilate wanting only to ascertain whether Jesus claimed to be the ruler of the Jewish people (Mark 15:2–5; Matt. 27:11–14). That is, Pilate wanted to know whether Jesus challenged the emperor for control of the land of Israel. Perhaps Pilate feared an armed revolt. In any event, Jesus replied only, "You say so" and then was silent when the chief priests reiterated the charges against him.

Luke, by contrast, has the assembly tell Pilate that Jesus forbade the community to pay taxes to the emperor and that he called himself a monarch (Luke 23:2–5). These assertions are lies. Luke softens the picture of Pilate by having the governor declare that he can "find no basis for an accusation against" Jesus. However, the crowd became hostile, and Luke has Pilate send Jesus to Herod because some of the charges against Jesus stem from Galilee, where Herod has jurisdiction

(Luke 23:6–16). Neither Herod nor Pilate found Jesus guilty, so Pilate decided to flog and release Jesus.

Mark and Matthew then portray the custom (not mentioned in any sources in antiquity outside the Bible) of Rome releasing a prisoner. Incited by the chief priests, the crowd beseeches Pilate to release Barabbas (a murderer and insurrectionist) but to crucify Jesus (Mark 15:6–15; Matt. 27:15–26). Luke does not mention this custom, but has the crowd cry for Barabbas (Luke 23:17–25). By choosing Barabbas (a known killer) over Jesus (who renounces violence and teaches reconciliation with one's enemies) the crowd epitomizes the depth of evil in the old age. In these Gospels, the negative behaviors exhibited by traditional Jewish leadership in the trial of Jesus undermine confidence in that leadership.

In all three Gospels, Pilate declares Jesus' innocence. Yet, Pilate yields to the crowd's persistent cry, "Crucify him." By lacking the integrity to stand up for his conviction, Pilate represents the injustice of the old age.

Rome put people to death when the empire perceived the victims as threats to Roman rule. The fact that Jesus was crucified between two bandits (Mark 15:27; Matt. 27:38) supports the impression that Jesus was killed for insurrection. In a shameful irony, by caricaturing the Jewish role in the death of Jesus, the Gospel writers engage in a form of falsehood, the very accusation they make against the Jewish leaders in the death of Jesus.

The Crucifixion: The Realm of This World Does Its Worst

In those days, the upright part of the cross was left at the crucifixion site. The first three Gospels agree that an African, Simon of Cyrene (modern-day Libya), carried the beam of Jesus' cross (Matt. 27:32; Mark 15:21; Luke 23:26). Luke underscores that women were with Jesus the entire way (Luke 23:27–31).

Irony abounds in the stories of the death of Jesus. Mark and Matthew picture the soldiers mocking Jesus by dressing him as a ruler, not realizing that he is God's prime agent (Matt. 27:27–31; Mark 15:16–20). From the apocalyptic perspective, the sign "The King of the Jews" placed over Jesus on the cross has an element of truth (Mark 15:26; Matt. 27:37; Luke 23:37). Onlookers challenged Jesus to save himself, not realizing that after the resurrection, he would return on the clouds as part of the apocalypse that would save the world (Mark 15:22–32; Matt. 27:38–44; Luke 23:35–43).

The Gospel writers understood the darkness that hung over the land from noon until 3:00 p.m. as a darkness foreshadowing the collapse of the universe as part of the apocalypse (Mark 13:24–27; Matt. 24:29–31; Luke 21:25–28) and as signaling the incredible distance of the present world from the realm (Mark 15:33–41; Matt. 27:45–56; Luke 23:44–49). The tearing of the veil or curtain of the temple functioned similarly to anticipate the realm that contains no temple. Furthermore, by the time the Gospels were written, the temple was destroyed. The rending of the curtain meant that the community did not need the temple in order to be faithfully Jewish.

Death by crucifixion was slow and painful. The victim died by suffocation as the weight of the body gradually prevented the lungs from taking in air. The victim was sometimes lashed to the cross but sometimes spikes were driven through the wrists or (especially) through the lower leg or foot to hold the body motionless. The Romans held crucifixions in public areas so that the other people would see the fate of opponents of Rome. Victims could take several days to die. The death of Jesus in only three hours is thus relatively merciful.

All three Gospel writers anticipate Gentiles welcoming the gospel in their communities by having a Gentile centurion identify the dying Jesus. "Truly this man was God's Son." Jesus was buried according to Jewish practice. Matthew, by mentioning a guard at the tomb, emphasized that Jesus was indeed dead and his body was not stolen (Matt. 27:62–66).

The Meanings of Jesus' Death in the Gospels

Christians often interpret the death of Jesus as having saving significance in its own right. For example, Christians often say that Jesus' death was a sacrifice or that Jesus died in our place. Such themes do not surface in a forceful way in Mark, Matthew, or Luke, although they occur elsewhere in the Second Testament.[4] Some scholars think that the Suffering Servant of Isaiah (esp. Isa. 52:13–53:12) is in the background of the death of Jesus in these Gospels (e.g., Matt. 8:17; Luke 22:37). If so, the Gospel writers compare the situation of Jesus to that of Israel in exile (the Suffering Servant of Isaiah). Israel appeared to be defeated, but God promised to restore Israel, thereby not only vindicating Israel but using Israel's regeneration as a model for Gentiles of what God could do for them.[5] Similarly, the death of Jesus appears to be a defeat, but by raising Jesus from the dead, God shows that the promises of the new world are true. The communities of Mark, Matthew, and Luke invited Gentiles to participate in this new world.[6]

The most explicit interpretation of the death of Jesus in Mark and Matthew is to call it a "ransom" (Mark 10:45; Matt. 20:28). While occasional Christians think God or Jesus paid a ransom to the devil, such thinking is absent from the Gospels. In the first century, the notion of ransom invoked the idea of release from different forms of captivity.[7] In the framework of the Gospels, Jesus' death is a part of the process that leads to the release of the world from captivity to the old age. This way of thinking goes along with our interpretation of the Last Supper (above).

The Death of Jesus for Today

In my view, the death of Jesus as presented in Mark, Matthew, and Luke is not significant in and of itself but is important because it exposes the depth of evil in the present age. The Gospels present Jesus as offering the world the opportunity to repent and become a part of the movement toward the realm of God. However, forces in the old world are so threatened by the realm that they seek to eliminate its primary agent.

The death of Jesus can be a lens through which people today can continue to evaluate movements, circumstances, and other people. Where do we encounter values, behaviors, attitudes, and feelings that resist the realm? Where do we encounter individuals, groups, ideas, and systems that function for us much like Rome in these texts?

An increasingly common practice in Christian worship during Holy Week is for congregations to read extensively from the accounts of the last week of the life of Jesus without interpretive comments from the preacher. This practice is especially common on Palm Sunday. On the one hand, such raw reading has the benefit of helping the congregation encounter a significant portion of the Bible. On the other hand, the uninterpreted reading of the last week of the life of Jesus may leave the congregation with the impression that the portrayals of the Jewish people in these texts are accurate. In my view, Christians today should not simply read these stories but should correct their misrepresentations.

The suffering of Jesus is also a paradigm of the suffering of the disciples. After declaring that he will be betrayed and killed, Jesus asserts that the disciples must deny themselves and take up their crosses (Mark 8:27–9:1; Matt. 16:13–28; Luke 9:18–27). Jesus is not encouraging a morbid suffering neurosis nor is he speaking about suffering in general (such as the pain that accompanies illness). Jesus offers a pastoral warning that witness to the realm of God sometimes results in suffering. Indeed, such suffering will intensify amid the chaos of the last days.[8] For example, the disciples will be persecuted by authorities who do not welcome their witness to the realm.[9]

The idea of suffering because of one's witness was rooted in Judaism. The First Testament and other Jewish sources repeatedly articulate this motif.[10] Matthew acknowledges that the disciples will be persecuted "in the same way they persecuted the prophets who were before you" (Matt. 5:12). From this perspective, witnessing to the realm may involve communities in the risk of suffering. A Christian community today should consider the degree to which its members' witness to the realm might bring them into such conflict with contemporary authorities that the community might suffer.

Questions for Discussion

1. Review what you have heard and thought about the Jewish people and the death of Jesus over the years. Are some of your associations reminiscent of anti-Judaism?
2. The realm, of course, is an event that involves community. When you partake of the loaf and the cup, how does your congregation anticipate the realm?

3. Consider a recent decision in your congregation in the light of the behavior of the disciples in the last week of Jesus' life. Where did you see your congregation turning away from the realm in ways reminiscent of Judas, Peter, and the other disciples? Where did you see qualities that are more realm-like?

4. Keeping in mind the falsehood on the part of the Jewish leaders (and the Gospel writers) in connection with the trial of Jesus, can you identify some falsehoods that Christians perpetuate today?

5. What role does the death of Jesus play in your faith? How does that role compare and contrast with the way the death of Jesus functions in the Gospels?

6. What risks can you take in witnessing to the realm? Could such witness result in suffering? What could sustain you in such suffering?

The Resurrection: Definitive Sign of the Realm

*G*rowing up, I joined most other people in our congregation in believing that the Bible teaches that each person has an immortal and nonmaterial soul that leaves the body at death and goes either to be with God (heaven) or to punishment (hell). In Bible college I was surprised to learn that the idea of immortality of the soul is more characteristic of Greek thought than Hebrew, and that the dominant view in the Second Testament is resurrection from the dead—the idea that the self dies, loses consciousness, and is later brought back to life after the apocalypse.

And so for a time I thought that the Second Testament does not contain immortality of the soul but teaches resurrection from the dead. This dichotomy turned out to be too simple. Like most other scholars, I now recognize that lines between these two viewpoints are fluid, and that while the dominant perspective in the Second Testament leans toward resurrection, immortality of the soul is also present.[1] Nevertheless, resurrection from the dead is the mode through which to understand the resurrection of Jesus in Mark, Matthew, and Luke.

In this chapter we first consider the origins and significance of the idea of the resurrection of the dead, and then look briefly at how it appears in the writings of Paul and in the descriptions of the transfiguration of Jesus. Then we concentrate on the resurrection itself in Mark, Matthew, and Luke. In the next chapter, we expand on immortality of the soul in connection with the Gospel of John, where that view is more evident.

Belief in Resurrection at the Time of Jesus:
Definitive Quality of the Realm

Many Jewish apocalyptic thinkers in the ancient world anticipated the resurrection of the dead as part of the realm of God. Christians today sometimes talk about the resurrection of the dead as being escapist. However, many ancient people saw the resurrection of the dead as the pièce de résistance of the realm, for by raising the dead and incorporating the faithful into the realm, God would fulfill the promise of complete blessing that they were denied by life in the old age. Resurrected people would then participate forever in the new cosmic world of the realm. Many thinkers who accepted this idea also believed that the wicked would be raised to punishment. Resurrection is thus a key part of the embodiment of God's righteousness in the realm.

Jewish thinkers differed as to what happened between the moment of death and the resurrection. Some thought that the self went into a kind of intermediate state similar to sheol.[2] Others thought that when the body died, the self simply lost consciousness. In either case, such thinkers expected that, at the apocalypse, God would resurrect the body. In the resurrection, the self would have a new body, one that is not subject to the difficulties of the old creation.

Daniel gives the first full description of the resurrection body in the First Testament. "Many of those who sleep in the dust of the earth shall awake, some to everlasting life, and some to shame and everlasting contempt. Those who are wise shall shine like the brightness of the sky, and those who lead many to righteousness, like the stars for ever and ever" (Dan. 12:2–3). Those who have such bodies (including angels) are resurrected and are part of the realm.

The author of 2 Baruch, writing after the fall of the temple, sets the resurrection of the dead explicitly in the context of the renewed world.

And it will happen after this day which is appointed is over [the apocalypse] that both the shape of those who are found to be guilty as also the glory of those who have proved to be righteous will be changed. For the shape of those who now act wickedly will be made more evil than it is (now) so that they shall suffer torment. Also, as for the glory of those who proved to be righteous on account of my law, those who possessed intelligence in their life, and those who planted the root of wisdom in their heart—their splendor will then be glorified by transformations, and the shape of their face will be changed into the light of their beauty so that they may acquire and receive the undying world which is promised to them. (*2 Bar.* 51:1–3)[3]

At the climax of 1 Corinthians, Paul relates the question, "How are the dead raised? With what kind of body do they come?" Paul then gives the fullest description of the resurrection body in the Second Testament. All things (such as the sun, moon, and stars) have their own glory, and the resurrection body has its own glory. "What is sown [at death] is perishable, what is raised [at the resurrection] is imperishable. It is sown in dishonor, it is raised in glory. It is sown in weakness, it is raised in power. It is sown a physical body, it is raised a spiritual body" (1 Cor. 15:35–49).

The Resurrection of Jesus: Sign of the Realm

The Gospel writers present Jesus raising people from the dead during his ministry—Jairus's daughter (Mark 5:21–43; Matt. 9:18–26; Luke 8:40–56) and the child of the widow of Nain (Luke 7:1–17). Indeed, as we pointed out in chapter 6, raising from the dead is a category of miracle story. While these raisings are signs of the realm becoming manifest through Jesus, they were not true resurrections (e.g., Mark 9:9–13; Matt. 10:5–15; 11:2–5; Luke 7:18–30). These people would die again to await the general resurrection of the dead that would take place at the apocalypse.

Mark, Matthew, and Luke interpret Jesus as being God's representative, announcing and anticipating the realm. The resurrection of Jesus, then, is the definitive sign that the final manifestation of the realm is at hand. The resurrected Jesus does not actually appear in Mark, but in Matthew and Luke he appears in a resurrection body as just described.

To the surprise of many contemporary Christians, the Gospels contain another appearance of the resurrected Jesus. Jesus was on a mountain with Peter, James, and John and "was transfigured before them."

Jesus' clothing "became dazzling white, such as no one on earth could bleach them" (Mark 9:2–8; Matt. 17:1–8; Luke 9:28–36).

Why, although still on earth, did Jesus appear in a resurrected body for a few moments? Jesus had just given the disciples the difficult news that as Messiah (agent of the realm) he would suffer, and that they, too, would suffer (Mark 8:27–9:1; Matt. 16:16–28; Luke 9:18–27). The disciples (and the communities to whom the Gospels were addressed) knew that hard days were ahead. The transfiguration gave them a preview of Jesus as he would appear after the resurrection and when he returned at the apocalypse. This preview strengthens their confidence in the coming of the realm by showing them what is ahead: resurrection. The voice from the cloud said, "Listen to [Jesus]." The transfiguration confirmed the authority of what Jesus said about the realm throughout his ministry and particularly his teaching about his suffering and that of the disciples. The stories of the resurrection of Jesus per se functioned similarly for the congregations to whom the Gospels were written.

Mark: Empty Tomb and Unusual Ending

The Gospel of Mark appears to end at Mark 16:20. However, virtually all scholars today conclude that someone after Mark added the material that now appears as Mark 16:9–20. If the Gospel of Mark ends at 16:8, we can see that Mark tells the story of the empty tomb that presupposes the resurrection of Jesus but does not actually describe an appearance of Jesus.

When the Sabbath was over, Mary Magdalene, Mary the mother of James, and Salome went to the tomb to complete the burial rites by anointing Jesus (Mark 16:1–7). However, Jesus was not in the tomb. Instead, they were greeted by a figure in a white robe (probably an angel) who told them that Jesus had been raised and that they were to tell the disciples and Peter that Jesus was going ahead of them to Galilee, where they would see Jesus.

Christians today are often puzzled by the end of the Gospel of Mark. Instead of joyously running to tell the disciples and then heading toward Galilee, the women "fled from the tomb, for terror and amazement had seized them; and they said nothing to anyone, for they were afraid" (Mark 16:8) Why would Mark end the Gospel in this strange way? Galilee for Mark is not simply a geographical location but is any place the realm is manifest. Many interpreters think Mark crafted this ending to provoke the members of Mark's community to consider whether their witness to the gospel in their own setting is like that of the women or whether they are doing as the figure commands. Are they fearfully keeping silent, or are they witnessing to the coming of the realm amid the chaos of the land of Israel after the fall of Jerusalem? Mark obviously hopes that they will witness.

Matthew: Living Presence Empowering Mission

In chapter 4 we found that Matthew regards Jesus as Emmanuel, God with us, in the sense that the ministry of Jesus was a sign of the final manifestation of the realm and the accompanying judgment. Indeed, for Matthew, the ministry of Jesus indicated the transforming presence of the realm.

In Matthew, only two women went to see the tomb (Matt. 28:1–10). Matthew does not mention spices or their desire to anoint the body. An earthquake (an apocalyptic sign) accompanied an angel (described as having the appearance of someone from the realm) who rolled back the stone. The angel sent the women to Galilee to see Jesus, but unlike the women described in Mark, these women went quickly with joy to tell the disciples. Jesus met them and reinforced the directive to go to Galilee.

Matthew is quite specific about what happened in Galilee (Matt. 28:16–20). The risen Jesus tells the disciples that they are to make disciples of "all nations." Here the term *nation* probably refers to Gentiles (in the way that it often does in the First Testament). Throughout the first Gospel, Matthew has stressed that the realm is coming soon, and so people need to be prepared. Matthew's Jesus gives instructions in how to make disciples: by baptizing (a sign of repentance and also a mark of gathering into a community to await the apocalypse) and "teaching them to obey everything that I have commanded you," that is, the content of what Jesus has just said in the Gospel of Matthew.

The last words of Jesus are significant. "And remember, I am with you always, to the end of the age." The reference to "the end of the age" refers to the coming apocalypse, which will end the world as it is and unveil the realm in its completeness. The fact that Jesus is resurrected means that the anticipation of the realm will continue in the world through the continuing presence of Jesus until the second coming. The disciples could do what Jesus said (baptize and teach), empowered by Jesus' living presence.

Luke: The Risen Christ Known in the Breaking of Bread

In Luke, a group of women went to the tomb, and as in Mark they brought spices (Luke 24:1–12). They found the stone rolled away, went in, and suddenly two men in "dazzling clothes" said that Jesus was raised and then reminded the women that Jesus had told them what would happen. Guided by this tradition, the women immediately went to tell others.

The women are the first preachers of the resurrection. However, their report seemed "an idle tale" to the other followers. Luke thus subtly impresses upon readers the trustworthiness of women. The actions of the women exercising leadership were, for Luke, an indication that God through the realm was restoring the relationships between women and men in community. Peter went to the tomb and saw only the grave cloths.

Later that day, two disciples were walking to Emmaus (Luke 24:13–35). Jesus walked with them but prevented them from recognizing him. The disciples had heard that women had reported that Jesus was alive but that when others went to the tomb, they did not see Jesus. The travelers were perplexed. Jesus began to teach the meaning of his ministry from Scripture. Luke's obvious point is that the community can understand the ministry of Jesus only by interpreting it through the First Testament.

As night fell, they ate. "When [Jesus] was at the table with them, he took bread, blessed and broke it, and gave it to them. Then their eyes were opened, and they recognized him." The words *took, blessed, broke,* and *gave* show that Luke has the Lord's Supper in mind. For Luke (as for Matthew and Mark), the sacred meal is an anticipation of the realm that explicitly includes experience of the risen Jesus with them.

The risen Jesus appeared to other followers (Luke 24:36–49). Jesus instructed the disciples to proclaim repentance and forgiveness to the nations, and to await the Holy Spirit. For Luke, the Holy Spirit is the force that animates the community in witness to the realm as they await the return of Jesus, whose ascension is related as the Gospel of Luke closes.

The Resurrection for Today

When teaching in local congregations, I am often asked, Did the resurrection of Jesus actually occur as it was reported in the Bible? The stories of the resurrection come from the apocalyptic worldview (see chap. 3), which is very different from the somewhat scientific worldview of most people in North America today. While the resurrection of Jesus made sense in the worldview of the first century, the idea of resurrection is not as much at home in the thought of many people in North America today. My perspective is that we cannot have irrefutable proof that the body of Jesus was resurrected. However, we do know from the Gospels that many people in the first century CE experienced Jesus alive after his death.[4] Indeed, I myself experience the living presence of Jesus when I partake of the loaf and the cup and at many other moments of life.

I have come to join some others in thinking that the stories of the resurrection are a first-century way of speaking about an abiding perspective that transcends both ancient and contemporary worldviews. The resurrection as sign of the presentation of the realm in the Gospels is a way of asserting that the power of life and renewal persists even in the face of destruction and death. The awareness of Jesus alive means that the power of the realm is still at work. In every moment of every situation, God seeks to lure the world toward a greater experience of love, justice, community, and abundance.

The question behind the question of whether the resurrection of Jesus actually occurred is often this: Will *we* live beyond the grave? Many people yearn to reunite with loved ones. Some people want to know whether they can have confidence that their immortal souls will go to heaven. Others want to know whether they will be resurrected. Some are not concerned about the mechanics (immortality or resurrection) but would like to anticipate some form of life beyond the grave. Again, we cannot *know* whether such life awaits. However, I believe that the faithfulness of God that we experience in this present life indicates that God can be trusted with whatever lies ahead.[5]

Questions for Discussion

1. In the past, how have you thought that the Bible conceived of life beyond the grave? Immortality of the soul? Resurrection of the dead? Have you thought the Bible conceived of some other way of thinking? Does this chapter alter your thinking? If so, how?

2. According to Mark, the risen Jesus is going ahead of the disciples to Galilee, where they will experience the fullness of the realm. How do you believe Jesus is going ahead of your congregation? Where is Jesus leading?

3. According to Matthew, the resurrection means that Jesus continues to be present, an empowering witness to the realm, especially to the reunion of all people. How can your congregation become more of a community that embodies such a reunion?

4. According to Luke, when a community gathers and breaks the bread, the risen Christ becomes known. Can you describe such an occurrence in your congregation?

5. The resurrection is the definitive sign of the coming of the realm. Where do you say resurrection is taking place today among individuals, communities, and social systems?

Jesus in the Gospel of John

Many Christians say that the Gospel of John is their favorite Gospel. Congregations sometimes urge new Christians to read the Gospel of John before reading the others because John is easier to understand. The Gospel of John, sometimes called the Fourth Gospel, contains some of the most beloved words and images of Jesus. For example, here we encounter "For God so loved the world" (John 3:16), and Jesus as the good shepherd (John 10:1–18). Focusing on Jesus from the perspective of John is a move into familiar territory. Yet even this Fourth Gospel holds its surprises and difficulties.

The Gospel of John differs from the Gospels of Mark, Matthew, and Luke in several respects. The picture of Jesus as revealer of God in the Gospel of John is quite different from Jesus as agent of the apocalyptic realm. Indeed, the notion of a coming realm has a low profile in the Fourth Gospel. In John Jesus speaks frequently (and often at great length) about his own identity (e.g., "I am the bread of life"), whereas in the first three Gospels Jesus speaks much more about the realm of God than about himself. John refers to the miracles of Jesus as signs and uses them in a special way. Whereas Jesus speaks mainly in crisp statements in the first three Gospels, in John Jesus typically teaches in long, sonorous, almost poetic discourses. Although parables are one of the most characteristic features of Jesus' speech in the first three Gospels, the Fourth Gospel does not contain a single parable. In John even the chronology of the story of Jesus is different from that in Mark, Matthew, and Luke. Because of such differences, many scholars today think the

Fourth Gospel goes even farther than the first three Gospels in presenting a particular interpretation of Jesus.

In this chapter, then, we look at the *Johannine* Jesus. As background, we first consider the two-story worldview presumed by the Gospel of John. We pause over John's relationship to Judaism and John's use of the expression "the Jews," and then unfold John's distinctive picture of Jesus.

The Two-Story Worldview of the Gospel of John

The worldview of the Gospel of John is quite different from the apocalyptic thinking found in Mark, Matthew, and Luke. John is written from the perspective of forms of Judaism that were influenced by Greek philosophical thinking that held that the universe is divided into two spheres—the sphere of heaven and the sphere of the world. While we can rightly speak of these spheres in spatial terms (heaven is above, the world is below), the heavenly sphere could penetrate the world. Sometimes Christians today also think of the world as a material sphere (e.g., flesh) and heaven as a nonmaterial one (spirit) but again, this separation is overstated. The nonmaterial could take expression in the material. After the writing of the Second Testament, a group called the gnostics would say that the material world is evil and the heavenly world is good and that the goal of religion was to free people from the evil material world (see chap. 11), but we should not read this absolute dichotomy into the Fourth Gospel.[1]

For John, the spheres of heaven and earth are marked by opposite qualities, as we can see in the following comparison:

Heaven	World
Life (eternal life)	Death
Love	Hate
Truth	Falsehood
Sight	Blindness
Fullness	Hunger
Freedom	Slavery
Oneness	Division

Heaven (*continued*)	**World** (*continued*)
Belief	Unbelief
Saved	Condemned
Born of God	Born of human will
Those who do what is true	Those who do evil
Recognize Jesus as revealing God	Do not recognize Jesus as revealing God

For John, the world (the cosmos) is thus not simply the earth and the seas and the sky as God created them in Genesis 1–2 but is a broken sphere in need of redemption. Jesus went from heaven into the world. As we note below, John's interpretation of Judaism and Jewish leaders is ambiguous: some Jewish leaders reflect the heavenly sphere, but others are decidedly of the world.

Moving back and forth between the first three Gospels and the Gospel of John can be a little confusing because they all presume a contrast between the way things are and the way they can be. For Mark, Matthew, and Luke, the contrast is one of time as well as of experience. At a future time, the present evil age will finally and fully give way to the realm. John gives very little attention to the end of the present cosmos and the beginning of a new cosmos but hopes that people experience the heavenly sphere in the present.[2] For John, while human beings are alive in the world, they can be animated by heaven. We can represent this situation in the following diagram.

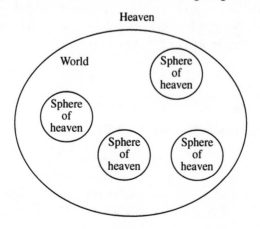

In the world, these different spheres exist alongside one another. The Gospel of John offers people the choice of living either in the sphere of heaven or in the sphere of the world. People can experience the sphere of heaven (life, light, etc.) in the present by believing in Jesus. However, in the present they will also experience difficulty and conflict, especially from those who do not believe. The complete experience of heaven comes only after death when the self goes to be with God (John 5:25–29; 14:1–13).

The Gospel of John, Judaism, and "the Jews"

With respect to Judaism and Jewish people, the Gospel of John is in an odd situation. On the one hand, Judaism is the source of virtually all of John's language and imagery about God, Jesus, and heaven. From this perspective, the Fourth Gospel is very Jewish. Indeed, one cannot fully understand Jesus in John without understanding Jewish language and perspectives.

On the other hand, John makes frequent negative reference to "the Jews." Scholars today agree that the writer of John does not include every Jewish person in antiquity in the phrase "the Jews," but refers to Jewish leaders and synagogues that oppose the Jesus movement. John sometimes uses "the Pharisees" synonymously with "the Jews."

The prevailing scholarly consensus is that the Johannine community had been part of a synagogue until conflict arose between them and other synagogue members regarding how to understand Jesus as an interpreter of God. According to John 9:22 and 9:34, the traditional synagogue has excommunicated the Johannine group.[3]

Ironically, the members of the Johannine community are Jewish. Moreover, the Fourth Gospel pictures Jesus as a rabbi instructing the disciples. From this perspective we can speak of the Johannine group as the Johannine synagogue. John's congregation offers an interpretation of how the God of Israel relates to the world that competes with the Jewish vision offered in the traditional synagogue down the street. The conflict is not between the new Christian religion and the old Jewish one but between two Jewish groups. Indeed, John tells the story of Jesus in the Fourth Gospel in such a way as to reinforce the identity of a beleaguered community by assuring them that they are

faithful Jews. For John, Jesus is the most reliable interpreter of God
and of Jewish tradition.

Jesus Reveals God

The Fourth Gospel, like the first three, is theocentric. That is, John
regards Jesus not as a religious end in himself but as one who reveals
God. Indeed, the most important work of Jesus in the Fourth Gospel
is to reveal God or to make God known. Jesus is able to reveal God
because Jesus was the Word who was with God before the creation of
the world, and indeed, Jesus was the agent through whom God created the world (John 1:1–4). Jesus functions so much like wisdom in
the Fourth Gospel that some scholars think John used wisdom as a
model for interpreting Jesus (or even that Jesus was an extension of
wisdom) (see Prov. 8:22–31; Wis. 7:22–8:1).

Jesus has "come down from heaven" into the world to reveal God
(e.g., John 3:13; 6:33–58; 15:15; 17:6, 26). As John says, "No one
[that is, no human being] has ever seen God. It is God the only Son,
who is close to the Father's heart, who has made him known" (1:18).
John suggests that while some knowledge of God came through the
Jewish tradition, the revelation that came through Jesus is fuller (e.g.,
John 1:17–18; 6:49–50; 8:39–47).

What is the content of Jesus' revelation? The best-known verse in
the Fourth Gospel summarizes this revelation. "For God so loved the
world that he gave his only Son, so that everyone who believes in him
may not perish but may have eternal life" (John 3:16). While Christians sometimes assume that the notion of God giving Jesus refers to
the crucifixion, in the Gospel of John the act of giving refers to the
whole event of Jesus descending from heaven, teaching and working
signs, and being crucified and resurrected.

In revealing God, Jesus reveals love, life, truth, sight, fullness, and
abundance. In making known these things, Jesus makes God known.
These qualities are characteristics of existence that come from the
heavenly sphere and take shape in the world. Life, for instance, is not
simply a matter of biology, but is the quality of existence that embodies the characteristics of heaven. Those who have life in the Johan-

nine sense experience and express God's love; they know the truth; they can see; their lives are full and abundant. By bringing the light of revelation into the world, Jesus exposes death, hate, falsehood, blindness, and hunger.

The relationship between Jesus and God is very close. Scholars agree that John does not see Jesus as a second God, and John does not have the full-blown doctrine of the Trinity in mind. However, scholars disagree on whether John regards Jesus as God or as God's closest agent (and revealer). Whether or not the Fourth Gospel presents Jesus as God or as God's revealer, the underlying confirmation is that the message that comes through Jesus is a trustworthy revelation of God.

The Signs Reveal Jesus

The Gospel of John recounts twelve miracles. However, John calls them not miracles but signs: for example, changing water into wine (2:1–11), healing an official's child (4:46–54), healing a person paralyzed for thirty-eight years (5:1–47), feeding the five thousand (6:1–15, 22–71), walking on the water (6:16–21), opening the eyes of a person born blind (9:1–41), and raising Lazarus from the dead (11:1–57). The function of the signs is to reveal that Jesus is the revealer whose words and actions are trustworthy representations of God. They also embody the nature of the revelation itself by pointing to what the heavenly world is like.

Several of the signs become occasions for revelatory encounters, with the focus less on the sign itself and more on Jesus speaking at length with other people. Jesus' words, of course, are revelation, and often the revelation both exhibits what God offers the world and criticizes the incomplete understanding of some Jewish people. The Sabbath healing of the person paralyzed for thirty-eight years is such a case (John 5:1–15). Immediately after the healing, some Jewish people began to persecute Jesus for healing on the Sabbath. They thought that Jesus had made himself equal with God. (vv. 16–18). This objection gave Jesus the opportunity to explain the nature of his authority. "Very truly, I tell you, the Son can do nothing on his own, but only what he sees the Father doing; for whatever the Father does, the Son does likewise" (v. 19). Readers can see the present-tense quality of experience of the sphere of heaven when Jesus says, "Very truly, I tell you, anyone who hears my word and believes [the one] who sent me has eternal life, and does not come under judgment, but has passed from death to life" (John 5:24). Jesus then criticized the Jews for not embracing him and for not knowing their own tradition well enough to recognize that Moses wrote about him (vv. 31–47).

The "I Am" Sayings Reveal Jesus

A distinctive feature of the Fourth Gospel is the "I am" sayings in several discourses of Jesus.

> "I am the bread of life" (John 6:35).
> "I am the light of the world" (8:12).
> "I am the gate for the sheep" (10:7).
> "I am the good shepherd" (10:11).
> "I am the resurrection and the life" (11:25).
> "I am the way, and the truth, and the life" (14:6).
> "I am the true vine" (15:1).

In almost every case, the Johannine Jesus applies to himself a quality that identifies him with the experience of Israel in the First Testament or in other Jewish literature. These qualities refer not just to Jesus but to the experience of the community that believes in him. As they believe, for instance, they experience the way to heaven.

These sayings (like many other elements in John) have a dual purpose. On the one hand, they assure the Johannine community that they are indeed still faithful to Jewish tradition. For example, when people believe in Jesus as the light of the world and belong to the synagogue of his followers, the Johannine community participates in the vocation of Israel as being the light of the world (e.g., Isa. 42:6). On the other hand, the "I am" sayings often have a polemical edge. Jesus affirms to a crowd of Jewish people, "I am the light of the world. Whoever follows me will never walk in darkness but will have the light of life" (John 8:12). In the ensuing interaction between Jesus and the crowd, the Gospel of John makes it apparent that these Jewish people (who do not believe in Jesus) are still walking in darkness. John has

Jesus say to them, "You are from your father the devil, and you choose to do your father's desires" (John 8:44).

The Core of the Teaching of Jesus: Love One Another

When the time came for Jesus to leave the world, Jesus washed the feet of the disciples, foretold his betrayal, and explained that the disciples could not immediately go where he was going. As was commonplace with other leaders in antiquity, Jesus gave his followers a final teaching, which we sometimes call his farewell discourse or last will and testament (14:1–17:26). The core of this teaching is that the disciples are to love one another in the way that Jesus loved them (13:34–35; 15:12; 15:17). In antiquity love was seen less as an emotion and more as the resolve to work for the good of another person. In the Gospel of John, Jesus expresses love by revealing God to the world. The disciples are to work for the good of one another and the community.

Jesus in the Gospel of John for Today

When I teach the Gospel of John in Bible study groups, I find that Christians typically have three responses to it. First, people are often attracted to the worldview of the Gospel of John. The idea of different spheres or qualities of perception operative helps many Christians explain their experience of life, especially as they realize that the spheres are not defined as particular spaces but refer to qualities of existence. They are aware that existence in the present can have the character of Johannine life just as it can have the character of Johannine death.

Second, they are attracted to the direct way that the Gospel speaks about love. Many people in North America have a deep yearning to experience unconditional love. The Gospel of John assures the congregation that God loves them and that God loves the world. Furthermore, in fractious and often confusing North America (and the broader world setting), Jesus' directive to love one another provides guidance for Christians as we think about how to love in personal and public situations.

Third, an increasing number of Christians are troubled by the negative portrayal of the Jews in the Gospel of John. Indeed, the picture of the Jewish authorities in John is the most negative of all the four Gospels. Many Christians recognize a contradiction in John between the call to love one another (to work for the good of others) and John's defamation of Jewish leaders.

Questions for Discussion

1. Make a list of the words and images of Jesus that come to mind most readily for you. Which ones are from the Gospel of John? What role has this Gospel played in your understanding of Jesus?

2. How do you react to the fact that the first three Gospels present a view of Jesus and of God's relationship to the world that differs from that of the Fourth Gospel?

3. To what degree do you experience the world in the way that John describes—as a sphere of death, hate, falsehood, blindness, and hunger? Do you experience the sphere of heaven in the midst of the world? What occurrences facilitate the experience of heaven in the midst of the world?

4. How do people in your congregation express Johannine-style love for one another? What could you do to enhance the expression of such love in your community?

11

Jesus in Gospels outside the Bible

The four Gospels in the Bible—Mark, Matthew, Luke, and John—were not the only books telling the story of Jesus written in the first two centuries CE.[1] We have already mentioned a collection of Jesus' sayings known as Q that was incorporated in Matthew and Luke. Churches wrote other Gospels. This chapter considers some examples—*Gospel of the Nazarenes, Gospel of the Ebionites, Gospel of Thomas, Gospel of Mary,* and *Gospel of Peter.* Many other similar materials survive from antiquity—Gospels, infancy narratives, and other partial Gospels as well as stories and letters associated with other apostles, such as the *Gospel of Philip, Gospel of the Egyptians,* the *Secret Gospel of Mark,* the *Infancy Gospel of Thomas,* the *Acts of Paul and Thecla,* the *Shepherd of Hermas,* the *Apocalypse of Peter.*[2]

This chapter first considers the character of these little-known Gospels and why they are not in the Bible. Then we will look at the beliefs or circumstances that generated several of these Gospels and summarize what they tell of the story of Jesus.

One aspect of this discussion can be a little confusing. The Gospels not found in the Bible are often called the apocryphal Gospels. (In Greek, the word *apocrypha* means "hidden.") The title "The Apocrypha" refers to a body of literature consisting of Jewish books written before the time of Jesus (such as Wisdom of Solomon, 1 and 2 Maccabees, and Sirach). The apocryphal *Gospels* are not included in the Apocrypha but are part of a larger apocryphal literature that deals with Jesus and the early church and includes not only apocryphal Gospels but also apocryphal acts and epistles.

Differences between Gospels Included
and Not Included in the Bible

These books are quite different not only from the four Gospels in the Bible but also from one another. The apocryphal Gospels are not simple biographies but tell the story of Jesus from the perspectives of the different communities that wrote them. Each Gospel presents a different understanding of Jesus. Some of these Gospels tell stories about his birth, youth, and resurrection that are not found in the Bible. Some congregations in the first centuries of the Common Era regarded these books as sacred Scripture much as congregations today look upon Mark, Matthew, Luke, and John.

Why are these Gospels not included in the Bible?[3] The same question can be asked of dozens of other books written by early Christian communities that we do not have in the Bible today. The short answer is that the mainstream of the church regarded them as presenting untrustworthy portraits of Jesus. To choose which Gospels to regard as authoritative, the church gradually developed informal criteria for ascertaining which Gospels (and other books) to recognize. These criteria are (1) consistency with the faith of the apostles (as determined by the churches making these decisions!), (2) wide use by early communities of followers of Jesus, and (3) the fact that they were quoted with authority by other ancient writers. The content of the Second Testament (as we know it) was not settled until 367 CE, when a bishop named Athanasius wrote a famous letter listing the twenty-seven books of the Second Testament as we have them today.[4]

Gospel of the Nazarenes

The *Gospel of the Nazarenes* was written by a group of Jewish followers of Jesus about the beginning of the second century CE. This Gospel presents Jesus as a righteous Jewish person whom God chose as Messiah, and it stresses the importance of following Torah (the law). Many of the sayings of Jesus in the *Gospel of the Nazarenes* are similar to those in the Gospel of Matthew. The *Gospel of the Nazarenes* does not contain stories of the birth of Jesus.

We can see the emphasis on following Torah in the *Gospel of the Nazarenes* in its version of the encounter between Jesus and a person of wealth.

> Another rich [person] said to him, "Master, what good thing shall I do to live?" [Jesus] said to [that person], "O [person], fulfill the law and the prophets." [The wealthy person] replied, "I have done that." [Jesus] said to him, "Go sell all that you possess and distribute it to the poor, and come, follow me." But the rich [person] began to scratch his head and it did not please him. And the Lord said to him, "How can you say, 'I have fulfilled the law and the prophets,' since it is written in the law, 'You shall love your neighbor as yourself,' and, lo! many of your [kinfolk], [children] of Abraham, are clothed in filth, dying of hunger, and your house is full of many goods and nothing at all goes out of it to them?" (*Gos. Naz.* 1)[5]

Jesus diagnosed this wealthy person's problem as failing to live up to the possibilities of Torah. Some scholars think that as tensions escalated between the followers of Jesus and traditional Jewish communities, the pervasive emphasis on following Torah in this Gospel was a primary reason leaders in the early church turned away from it.

Gospel of the Ebionites

At the beginning of chapter 1, I mentioned the custom of harmonizing the Gospels. Instead of acknowledging that the four canonical Gospels present four different stories of Jesus, harmonizers try to show that the apparent differences are not real differences but can be harmonized, that is, the Gospels can be put together to tell a single, continuous story. As far as we know the *Gospel of the Ebionites* was the first harmony. Like the community that wrote the *Gospel of the Nazarenes*, the Ebionites were Jewish followers of Jesus.

We can see the harmonizing tendency of the *Gospel of the Ebionites* at work in its account of the baptism of Jesus.

> After the people had been baptized, Jesus came also, and was baptized by John. And as he came out of the water, the heavens

opened, and [Jesus] saw the Holy Spirit descending in the form of a dove and entered into him. And a voice was heard from heaven, "You are my beloved Son, in whom I am well pleased." And again, "This day have I begotten you." And suddenly a great light shone in that place. And John, seeing [Jesus], said, "Who are you, Lord?" Then a voice was heard from heaven, "This is my beloved Son, in whom I am well pleased." Thereat John fell at his feet and said, "I pray you, Lord, baptize me." But [Jesus] would not, saying, "Suffer it, for thus it is fitting that all should be accomplished." (*Gos. Eb.* 4)[6]

In each account of the baptism of Jesus in the Gospels in Mark, Matthew, and Luke, the voice from heaven speaks only one time. The *Gospel of the Ebionites* has the voice from heaven speak three times—once each for the accounts from Mark, Matthew, and Luke!

In addition to underlining the importance of following Torah, one of the distinguishing characteristics of the community that wrote this Gospel was the practice of vegetarianism. They became vegetarian because they believed that the sacrifice of Jesus ended the need for other sacrifices. In the ancient world, most meat sold in the marketplace had been sacrificed to a god (by way of the seller pinching off a little piece of the meat and placing it on an altar). The Ebionites sought to avoid complicity with sacrifice by becoming vegetarian. That is why they changed the diet of John the Baptist from locusts and wild honey to the following. "And [John's] meat was wild honey, which tasted like manna, formed like cakes of oil" (*Gos. Eb.* 2).[7] John ate honey and cakes, not locusts and honey.

Gospel of Thomas

The *Gospel of Thomas* is probably the best known of the nonbiblical Gospels. It does not contain a narrative of the life of Jesus but consists of 114 "secret teachings" that are attributed to Jesus. In its present form, the *Gospel of Thomas* presumes a gnostic worldview. The word *gnostic* is from a Greek word for knowledge. The gnostics believed that existence was divided into two parts—the good nonmaterial dimension and the evil material dimension. They conceived of God as a nonmaterial spirit and the heavenly world as nonmaterial dimension. A human being was made up of two parts—the body (material) and the soul (nonmaterial), with the soul trapped or entombed in the body. Salvation could take place when the body attained the knowledge (*gnosis*) that would enable the soul to leave the body and to enter the nonmaterial world of heaven. This knowledge was a secret, a mystery, and could only be gained from a teacher or revealer.

The *Gospel of Thomas* portrays Jesus as the source of revelatory knowledge that allows the soul to leave the body and to join God in heaven. Here is one of the sayings of Jesus from this Gospel that is similar to many others representing this viewpoint.

> Jesus said, "I took my place in the midst of the world, and I appeared to them in the flesh. I found all of them intoxicated; I found none of them thirsty. And my soul became afflicted for [the children of humankind] because they are blind in their hearts and do not have sight; for empty they came into the world, and empty too they seek to leave the world. But for the moment they are intoxicated. When they shake off their wine, then they will repent." (*Gos. Thom.* 28)[8]

Jesus came down from heaven in a body ("in the flesh") in order to impart knowledge. When *Thomas* refers to finding people intoxicated, the Gospel has in mind not people who are drunk but people who think that life has only a material dimension. They are not thirsty for the nonmaterial world. They came empty and desire to leave empty, that is, their experience in the world is of no benefit. However, when they receive the sight that Jesus gives (and are no longer blind), they will repent; that is, they will recognize a need for the secret knowledge that Jesus can give them, which will lift them into the heavenly world.

Some scholars think that the *Gospel of Thomas* contains some sayings of Jesus that are older than their counterparts in the biblical Gospels. For instance, *Thomas* gives a much shorter version of the parable of the Mustard Seed than does the Gospel of Mark (*Gos. Thom.* 20; Mark 4:30–32). Nevertheless, the sayings in *Thomas* are so few and so void of historical context from the life of Jesus that they cannot generate a complete picture of Jesus. As I once heard a major biblical scholar ask, "How can you build an entire picture of Jesus out of a few aphorisms?"

Gospel of Mary

Christians whose imaginations have been fueled by contemporary popular fiction about the relationship between Jesus and Mary will likely be disappointed by the *Gospel of Mary*. Only fragments of this short book have survived, and like the *Gospel of Thomas*, they are gnostic. The *Gospel of Mary* consists of two main parts. One part is a dialogue between the disciples and the risen Jesus concerning matter and sin. For example, in a comment that shows the gnostic background of this Gospel, Jesus says, "Matter gave birth to a passion which has no Image because it derives from what is contrary to nature" (*Gos. Mary* 3).[9]

The other part of the *Gospel of Mary* consists of Mary comforting the other apostles and receiving a vision describing the ascent of the soul. The closing words of her vision are also self-evidently gnostic. "What binds me has been slain, and what surrounds me has been destroyed. . . . In a word, I was set loose for a world and in a type, from a type, which is from above" (*Gos. Mary* 9).[10]

After Mary recounts her vision, some of the disciples protest. Andrew thinks that Jesus never said what Mary reports. Peter is aghast that Jesus would give preferential revelation to a woman (*Gos. Mary* 10). This interchange may suggest that some gnostic groups had women leaders (represented by Mary) and that other gnostics attacked these communities and their women leaders (the attackers represented by Andrew and Peter). If so, unfortunately we do not know how the conflicts turned out.

Gospel of Peter

The *Gospel of Peter*, which also has something of a gnostic quality, was used as scripture by some congregations in the second century. As the title implies, this book purports to be the story of Jesus as told by Peter; however, no scholar today believes that this was the case. This document, like so many others in antiquity, was pseudonymous.

The actual author was an anonymous writer who attributed the book to a well-known figure in order to add to the authority of the book. We do not possess a complete text of this Gospel but have only the part that focuses on the death and resurrection of Jesus.

The *Gospel of Peter* intensifies the negative portrayal of the Jewish people in the death of Jesus, thus suggesting that the community that wrote this Gospel was in extreme tension with elements of Judaism. This motif is evident from the first words of the surviving part of this Gospel. Evidently recalling Pilate washing his hands of the death of Jesus, Peter says, "But none of the Jews washed their hands, neither Herod nor any of his judges" (*Gos. Pet.* 1).[11] Herod then gives the order for Jesus to be crucified.

After the crucifixion, Jesus was buried. A large group of people come to see the tomb but the stone rolls away by itself. Three people come out of the tomb, two of them tall enough that their heads extend into heaven while the head of the third one goes beyond heaven. A cross walks out of the tomb after them. A heavenly voice asks whether the cross has preached to the people who are sleeping. When the cross responds with a yes, some of the observers report this event to Pilate, prompting the Jewish officials to want to silence the story because they are afraid other Jews will want to put them to death when they realize how wrong the officials were in putting Jesus to death. "For it is better for us," they said, "to make ourselves guilty of the greatest sin before God than to fall into the hands of the people of the Jews and be stoned" (*Gos. Pet.* 34–49).[12]

The Importance of the Apocryphal Gospels Today

The church today does not need the apocryphal Gospels in order to develop an adequate understanding of Jesus. However, awareness of these Gospels can be helpful to the church today in two ways.

First, the apocryphal Gospels give us a broader picture of the diversity of the early Christian communities than we find in the Bible. Christians today sometimes look back with nostalgia at the first century of the Common Era, thinking that the early church was a pristine community in which everyone had the same harmonious thoughts. The apocryphal Gospels give us windows not only into different

views of Jesus but into even greater diversity in the early church—
different theologies, different ways the early communities worshiped
and prayed, and different attitudes and actions toward the state, sex-
uality, family life, and even willingness to die for one's faith. In these
matters, the early churches were as diverse as Christian denominations and movements today.

Second, as I noted in the preface to this book, the church today is
divided into many camps regarding how to interpret Jesus. The presence of the apocryphal Gospels (along with the fact of having four different Gospels included in the Bible) reminds us that from the earliest
days, Christian communities have put forward diverse pictures of
Jesus. Churches today need not be discouraged by the fact that we
struggle with different ways of perceiving Jesus; they can recognize
that searching for how to interpret Jesus is a key part of what it means
to be Christian.

Such diversity indicates that we are called to do for our time what
the ancient communities did in their times (and what Christian communities have done in every era): we must search for the most adequate understandings of Jesus Christ for today. Even as we do so,
however, the fact of so many different Gospels reminds us that we can
never come to a full and complete knowledge of Jesus. Even our best
comprehensions of Jesus are incomplete. Consequently, today's
Christians should not brandish their perceptions of Jesus like swords
to cut down non-Christians and other Christians but should offer our
understandings in a spirit of humility and openness, recognizing that
the risen Jesus transcends all our awareness and formulations.

Questions for Discussion

1. Before reading this book, what did you know about these
   Gospels?
2. The stream of the early church that eventually became the mainstream used three criteria for determining which Gospels to recognize as authoritative: (a) consistency with the faith of the
   apostles; (b) cited widely by other ancient writers; (c) quoted
   with authority by other ancient writers. Which of these criteria—and what additional reasons—are most compelling to you

for continuing to recognize Mark, Matthew, Luke, and John as reliable guides for the church today?

3. Based on the pictures of Jesus in the nonbiblical Gospels summarized above, what do you find intriguing? What questions are raised for you by these Gospels?

4. How did (and does) the omission of these materials from the Bible help the church today? Can you imagine ways that keeping these Gospels out of the Bible has limited the church?

5. The communities that wrote the Gospels discussed in this chapter were attempting to tell the story of Jesus in ways that were at home in their assumptions, worldviews, and cultures. How might you tell the story of Jesus today in language and imagery that is at home in your culture?

The Life of Jesus for Today

As this book has unfolded, the closing remarks and the Questions for Discussion in nearly each chapter have reflected on the significance of aspects of the life of Jesus for today. For example, how can the teaching of Jesus help us today? What can we make of the miracle stories today? The time is now at hand to meditate in a broader way on the importance of the life of Jesus for today.

We will begin with a consideration of the fact that the Bible contains multiple pictures of Jesus, and of the problems and possibilities posed by these materials. I then distinguish between surface and deeper meanings of texts. This perspective opens the way to discuss what I take to be the most important aspect of the life of Jesus today—that Jesus points us to God. The chapter finishes with some thoughts about how the small size of the Jesus movement in antiquity could be a lens for locating expressions of that movement in the contemporary setting.

In the background of this chapter is an issue that came to the surface in chapter 1. Christians often want the life of Jesus to represent their own values and perspectives. The versions of the life of Jesus as described in this book probably differ from Jesus as many readers would like to find him. From my point of view, Jesus was an apocalyptic prophet and not just a guide to a more fulfilling middle-class life, nor a wisdom teacher, nor a social reformer, nor a person whose one agenda was opposing the Roman Empire. What can we say in a positive way today that is both faithful to the intentions of Jesus as he was in history (and as interpreted by the four Gospel writers) and that can help us come to a credible and faithful understanding of the purposes of God?

One Jesus and Four Gospels

The Second Testament contains two basic stories of the life of Jesus in the Second Testament. One story is told by Mark, Matthew, and Luke and depicts Jesus as an apocalyptic prophet who announces the end of the present age and prepares people for an apocalypse that will be the means whereby the realm of God comes to final and full expression. Virtually all aspects of the ministry of Jesus exhibit the realm. Mark, Matthew, and Luke each tell this basic story of Jesus from their own perspectives in order to address particular situations in the communities to which they wrote.

The Gospel of John tells the other basic story of Jesus from the standpoint of another worldview. John thinks of the universe as made up of a sphere of light and life (heaven) and a lower story of darkness and death (the world), with Jesus descending from heaven to reveal the ways of God, light, and life to those who live in the world of darkness and death.

Each Story of Jesus Has Possibilities and Problems

Each of the two basic ways of interpreting the story of Jesus presents today's Christian community with certain elements that are attractive and certain elements that are problematic. On the one hand, as we pointed out in chapter 3, the idea of a new realm is very inviting to many people who live in North America. Although few people experience the present world as entirely evil, distortions of human life— for example, racism, sexism, classism, ageism, sickness, suffering, and violence—are commonplace and make many people yearn for the world to have qualities that are associated with the realm.

On the other hand, Mark, Matthew, and Luke all supposed that they were living in the last days and that the apocalypse would occur soon. Almost two thousand years have passed, but the apocalypse has not taken place. Indeed, the social conditions that created the longing for the realm are magnified. Warfare, for instance, can destroy people, cities, and elements of nature on a scale unmatched in human history.

Some Christians deal with the fact that the realm has not come by saying that it is simply delayed. Perhaps Jesus did not understand God's time line. Perhaps, as we noted in chapter 3, "With God, one day is like a thousand years, and a thousand years are like one day" (see Ps. 90:4; 2 Pet. 3:8). However, many Christians note that the idea of an apocalyptic coming of the realm derives from a worldview that many people no longer share. They surmise that the nonarrival of the realm is not simply a delay but an indication that an apocalypse is not likely to occur. Furthermore some followers of Jesus today conclude that a God of unconditional love would not intentionally delay the second coming. How could God be pure unbounded love and actively permit suffering to continue? Jesus may have healed a few people in the ancient world as signs of the realm, but what do such signs mean to the human community today in which more people can be killed in a single rash of genocide than were alive in the whole of the eastern Mediterranean world at the time of Jesus?

Some Christians today find the worldview of the Gospel of John more attractive than the apocalyptic perspective of Matthew, Mark, and Luke. The idea of spheres of experience within a continuous universe makes more sense to such folk than the idea of one era of history dissolving in an apocalypse and being replaced by a renewed universe. However, John's view of existence is more static than the way in which many people experience life today. Many people today experience life in more complex and ambiguous ways than are explained by this simple dichotomy posed by John of living in either heaven or earth. Furthermore, we are troubled that the story of Jesus in John is mixed with the criticism of Judaism that permeates that book. Even if we understand such criticism as one Jewish group speaking about another, the criticism of traditional Judaism is so woven into John's narrative that many people today cannot affirm the entirety of the theology of the Fourth Gospel.

A Christian community cannot simply choose the pictures of Jesus in Mark, Matthew, and Luke over that of the Gospel of John (or vice versa). As we have just seen, while each picture has certain things that commend it, each picture also raises some difficult issues for the Christian community today.

Distinguishing between Surface and Deeper Meanings

One way to attempt to overcome the impasse between having multiple pictures of the life of Jesus in the Bible but finding none of them entirely satisfactory is to think of the language of the Bible as having both surface and deeper meanings.[1] At the surface level, what does a text ask you to believe and do? At the deeper level, what does a text ask you to believe and do? At each level, that is, what does a text invite you to believe as true about God and the world, and what does the text invite you to do in response?

The surface meaning of a story is the simple meaning of the story in its original worldview. The surface meaning assumes that the elements of the worldview within which the story is told are straightforward. For example the story of Jesus narrated by Mark asks us to believe that Jesus is an apocalyptic prophet who anticipated an apocalypse. In response, we are to repent and prepare for the apocalypse by witnessing to the realm, especially to Gentiles.

The deeper meaning of a text is the fundamental intention or function of the story that does not depend upon the surface elements of the story. To make an analogy, the relationship between the surface and deeper perspectives is like that of a husk and an ear of corn. The husk is the wrapping in which the ear of corn comes. But the ear itself is the essence of corn. The deeper meaning is the essential aspect of the story. The story is expressed in the language and imagery of a particular worldview, but the essence of the story is not limited to that worldview.

The Deeper Witness of the Story of Jesus

Both major stories of the life of Jesus in the Bible contain surface and deeper elements. The story of Jesus in Mark, Matthew, and Luke presumes that existence in its present condition is far from the purposes of God. While there are certainly moments for individuals and communities that embody love and mutual support, some aspects of life subvert or deny such purposes. However, the deeper witness of the expectation of a coming realm is that God is not satisfied with the world as it is but intends for people and nature to live together in conditions that optimize the well-being of all.

I like the way Clark M. Williamson summarizes the deeper witness of the story of Jesus (and of the Bible as a whole). This story, he says, testifies to God's unconditional love for each and all (including nature) and to God's unceasing will for justice for all. In this context, justice is the social form of love. God seeks for all people to experience unconditional love and for all people (and elements of nature) to live together in love.[2]

A major function of the first three Gospels is to assure communities who live in the broken world that God continues to be present to work toward greater experiences of love and justice. These Gospels give people hope in the midst of chaotic circumstances in the social world and in nature. The deeper meaning of the life of Jesus as told by the Gospel of John is very similar. John presumes that the world is a sphere in which the experience of life goes against the purposes of God. Existence in the world is marked by darkness, falsehood, misperception, violence, and death. However, God loves the world and acts through Jesus Christ to reveal how people in the world can experience love, life, light, truth, freedom, and abundance.

While John uses different language and a different set of concepts than Mark, Matthew, and Luke, their underlying ideas are quite similar. Both stories of Jesus assume that life in the present does not fulfill all of God's purposes for love, community, health, wholeness, justice, and abundance. They also present God as actively seeking to help the world move in the direction of embodying those qualities.

A key point is that both the first three Gospels and the Fourth Gospel regard Jesus as pointing to the larger work of God, which is to increase the experience of love in individual lives and in communal life. The focus is not upon Jesus himself (as it is in some churches today) but is upon how Jesus helps people in the world discern God's presence and purposes.

Most Christians today can join all four Gospel writers in thinking that life in the early twenty-first century is far from the way God would like it to be. We can surely also agree that God continues to desire that individuals and communities experience fuller lives that are characterized by love and justice. Furthermore, the resurrection confirms that Jesus continues to be present to assist the church in such discernment.

Interpreting Life Today in Light of Jesus Christ: Love and Justice

I admit a frustration that comes with the perspective on Jesus Christ developed in this book (and that accompanies many other approaches to the life of Jesus). While Jesus spoke directly about issues in his own day, and while the Gospel writers have adapted traditions about Jesus to specific issues in their settings after the fall of Jerusalem, Jesus did not speak directly about issues today, nor do the Gospels.

Toward the end of chapter 9, in connection with the resurrection, I articulated a perspective on identifying moments of resurrection today that can be enlarged to interpret life from the perspective of Jesus. When confronted with a personal matter or a congregational decision or an issue in the larger world, a Christian can ask,

> With respect to this issue, what perceptions and behavior are most consistent with God's unconditional love for each and all (elements of nature included) and with God's call for justice, that is, for all to live in social relationships of love?

An individual Christian or a Christian congregation can identify attitudes and actions that have the greatest likelihood of enhancing the well-being of the most people in the circumstances. The other side of this question is to ask,

> What attitudes and actions have the greatest likelihood of denying God's love to some individuals (or elements of nature) or of denying justice (or possibilities for right relationships) in a particular situation?

Such latter attitudes and actions are typically not consistent with the story of Jesus Christ for today.

This approach is not simply asking, What would Jesus do? While asking that question has the virtue of encouraging people to reflect on particular issues from the perspective of Jesus, the truth is that we cannot confidently know what Jesus would do in specific contemporary situations. The approach advocated in this chapter calls for Christians to analyze situations from the perspective of basic values that grow from the story of Jesus, which itself grows from the heart of the Jewish tradition.

Many people today yearn for clear and unambiguous guidance in how to witness faithfully. In some cases, this approach will generate forthright perspectives. For example, in every circumstance, capital punishment is inconsistent with the deepest aspects of the story of Jesus. However, to be candid, some things that happen in life are so ambiguous that it is not absolutely clear what perspectives and decisions express love and which ones do not. Christians may disagree with one another on how to interpret specific events. In some situations, the same decision may express love for some people but deny love to others. Christians must sometimes make decisions based on the *likelihood* that a particular choice will demonstrate more of God's love for a person or group than another choice.

The Small Size of the Movement in Antiquity as Lens for Today

Many Christians today think that the whole of the ancient world had its eyes on Jesus and the movement that came after him. As this book ends, however, I pause over the fact that Jesus' life (and the lives of his followers after the resurrection) attracted very little attention outside their immediate locations. We know of only two or three writers in the first century outside the Jesus movement who even referred to Jesus. The Roman Suetonius mentions a figure called Chrestus, whose followers were creating a disturbance in Rome.[3] The name Chrestus appears to be a misspelling of the Greek word for Christ. The Jewish writer Josephus mentions both John the Baptist and Jesus, as well as other figures such as the prophet Theudas.[4]

However, when seen in the ongoing story that begins in the First Testament, the small notice of Jesus and the Jesus movement is an important reminder. The First Testament consistently pictures God operating in the world in ways that appear to the imperceptive eye to be small and insignificant. Who would have thought that the Sovereign of the Universe would seek to bless the entire world by giving children to a couple (Sarai and Abram) old enough to be on Medicare? Who would have imagined that the people who were called to be the light to the world would be enslaved in Egypt or exiled in Babylon? Even when David ruled and the state was at the height of its political power, Israel was much smaller than the mighty nations around it. It is, therefore, no surprise that Jesus lived on the margins of antiquity.

This pattern of God seeking to bless the world through unlikely figures, communities, and movements can serve as a template for Christians today. It can cause us to ask, Who are unlikely people today witnessing to God's purposes for the world to become a place of unconditional love and justice? Who—individuals, communities, or movements—may unexpectedly point the way to regeneration and renewal? From this perspective, a study of the life of Jesus is a resource for the path to blessing.

Questions for Discussion

1. How would you respond to someone who says to you that the Bible contains just one picture of Jesus Christ? How (if at all) would this response differ from one that you would have made before making your way through these pages?

2. Now that you have read this book and have considered some possibilities and problems in thinking about Jesus Christ, write a paragraph describing how you understand Jesus Christ. Show your description to a companion and let that person interview you concerning what you believe about Jesus and how that belief should affect what you do.

3. Name an issue that is one of the most important facing you in your personal or household life. What choices offer the greatest possibility for expressing love for you and for others in the situation? Repeat this exercise with respect to your congregation and the world.

4. Where can you point to an individual or to a movement today that is small in size but that seems to you to witness to God's purposes for the world in a way that is similar to the Jesus movement?

5. As you leave this study, name at least one question that you still have regarding the life of Jesus as it took place in the world of the first century or as the Gospel writers (or others) interpreted

in that time. Name another question that is still in your mind or heart regarding the significance of Jesus for today. Think about resources to which you might turn to help you think about these issues, such as members of a Bible study group, published resources for interpreting the Bible (such as Bible commentaries or Bible dictionaries), or your minister (who would be thrilled to talk with you about serious biblical interpretation).

Notes

Chapter 1: Why a Book on the Life of Jesus?

1. Luke Timothy Johnson, *The Real Jesus: The Misguided Quest for the Historical Jesus and the Truth of the Traditional Gospels* (San Francisco: HarperSanFrancisco, 1996), 112.

Chapter 2: The World at the Time of Jesus

1. For examples of differing emphases, see Mark Allan Powell, *Jesus as a Figure in History: How Modern Historians View the Man from Galilee* (Louisville, KY: Westminster John Knox Press, 1998).
2. See, e.g., Richard A. Horsley, *Jesus and Empire: The Kingdom of God and the New World Disorder* (Minneapolis: Fortress Press, 2003), 23–24.
3. Josephus, *Jewish Antiquities. Books 18–19,* trans. Louis H. Feldman, Loeb Classical Library (Cambridge: Harvard University Press, 1965), 18.1.4, 18.16–17, pp. 13–15.
4. Ibid., 18.1.5, 18.18–23, 15–19.
5. Ibid., 18.1.6, 18.23–24, 21–23.

Chapter 3: The Realm of God

1. I prefer the term *realm* to other inclusive words that are replacements for *kingdom*, words such as *reign, dominion, domain, holy commonwealth,* or *kin-dom.* The word *realm* better captures the full-bodied sense of place, time, and activity.
2. For a description and defense of this approach, see Robert J. Miller, *The Jesus Seminar and Its Critics* (Santa Rosa, CA: Polebridge Press, 1999).
3. 2 Esdras (sometimes known as 4 Ezra) is easily accessible in the Apocrypha section of the Bible or in separate volumes containing the Apocrypha. The other apocalyptic writings are

accessible in James H. Charlesworth, ed., *The Old Testament Pseudepigrapha: Apocalyptic Literature and Testaments* (Garden City, NY: Doubleday & Co., 1983).
4. 1 Enoch 10:18–23, trans. E. Isaac, in Charlesworth, *Old Testament Pseudepigrapha*, 2:18–19.
5. Oscar Cullmann, *Christ and Time: The Primitive Christian Conception of Time and History* (Philadelphia: Westminster Press, 1950), 84.

Chapter 4: The Birth of Jesus and the Beginning of His Ministry

1. A classic study of the birth narratives is Raymond E. Brown, *The Birth of the Messiah*, updated ed. (Garden City, NY: Doubleday Anchor, 1999).

Chapter 5: Jesus, Judaism, and Conflict with Others

1. Although the Talmud was given its present form much later than the time of Jesus, it contains some materials that probably reflect conditions at the time of Jesus.
2. For an exceptionally clear statement of this perspective, see E. P. Sanders, *The Historical Figure of Jesus* (London: Penguin Books, 1993), 205–38.
3. E.g., M. Eugene Boring, *The Continuing Voice of Jesus: Christian Prophecy and the Gospel Tradition* (Louisville, KY: Westminster John Knox Press, 1991).
4. On this subject, see Clark M. Williamson, ed., *A Mutual Witness: Toward Critical Solidarity Between Jews and Christians* (St. Louis: Chalice Press, 1992).

Chapter 6: Realm Themes at the Center of the Teaching of Jesus

1. For such summaries, see E. P. Sanders, *Judaism: Practice and Belief, 63 BCE–66 CE* (London: SCM Press, and Valley Forge: Trinity Press International, 1992), 257–60.
2. *Testament of Dan* 5:3, from "Testaments of the Twelve Patriarchs," trans. H. C. Kee, in Charlesworth, *Old Testament Pseudepigrapha*, 2:809.
3. For fuller discussion, see Ronald J. Allen and Clark M. Williamson, *Preaching the Gospels without Blaming the Jews: A Lectionary Commentary* (Louisville, KY: Westminster John Knox Press, 2004), 17–28.

4. For a study of the parables from this perspective, see Dennis E. Smith and Michael E. Williams, eds., *The Storyteller's Companion to the Bible: The Parables of Jesus* (Nashville: Abingdon Press, 2006), vol. 11.

Chapter 7: Jesus Demonstrates the Realm through Miracles

1. For an excellent collection, see Wendy Cotter, *Miracles in Greco-Roman Antiquity: A Sourcebook for the Study of New Testament Miracle Stories* (London: Routledge, 1999).
2. *Ta'anit* 23A in Jacob Neusner, *The Babylonian Talmud: A Translation and Commentary* (Peabody, MA: Hendrickson, 2005), 7:120–22.
3. *Berakhot* 34B, in Neusner, *Babylonian Talmud,* 1:232–33.
4. *Baba Mesia* 59A, in Neusner, *Babylonian Talmud,* 14:287.
5. They confirm the authority of Jesus as agent of God (e.g., Mark 1:21–28; 2:1–12; 3:7–12; 3:19–30; 6:6–13; Matt. 11:7–19; 12:15–21; 12:22–32; Luke 6:17–19; 9:1–6; 11:14–16). They express God's compassion for those who receive them (Mark 6:34; Matt. 8:2; 9:36; 14:14; 15:32; 20:34; Luke 7:13). Some miracles become occasions for teaching (e.g., Mark 2:23–3:6; Matt. 8:5–13; 9:1–8; Luke 5:17–26).
6. Note that the word *follow* occurs in Matt. 8:18–22 and again in 8:23.
7. For a scholar in the liberal tradition who acknowledges the possibility of miracles today (without reducing them to a formula), see Bruce Epperly, "Miracles without Supernaturalism: A Process-Relational Perspective," *Encounter* 67 (2006): 47–62.
8. Antoinette Clark Wire, "The Structure of the Gospel Miracle Stories and Their Tellers," *Semeia* 11 (1978): 109–10.

Chapter 8: Rejecting the Realm

1. Cf. Mark 9:31–34; 10:33–41; Matt. 10:17–19; 17:22–23; Luke 9:43–45; 18:31–34.
2. Note especially Josephus's use of this term in H. Rengstorf, *Theological Dictionary of the New Testament,* trans. G. W. Bromiley (Grand Rapids: Wm. B. Eerdmans, 1967), vol. 4, 258–59, s.v. "lestes."
3. For Jewish trial procedures, see the fourth division of the Mishnah ("Damages," or *Nezikin*), in Jacob Neusner, *The Mishnah: A New Translation* (New Haven, CT: Yale University Press, 1991), 503–698.
4. E.g., Rom. 3:21–26; 5:6; 1 Cor. 15:3; Eph. 2:14–15; Col. 2:13–15; 1 Tim. 1:15; 2:6; Titus 2:14; Heb. 6:19–20; 7:27; 9:11–12; 10:10–12; 1 Pet. 1:18–19; 2:21–25; Rev. 1:5; 5:9–10; 7:14. These occurrences require careful interpretation from the perspective of their meanings in antiquity.

5. On Isa. 52:13–53:12, see Ronald J. Allen and Clark M. Williamson, *Preaching the Old Testament: A Lectionary Commentary* (Louisville, KY: Westminster John Knox Press, 2007), 40–42.
6. We could make similar comments about Pss. 22 and 69 and various other passages.
7. F. Büschel, *Theological Dictionary of the New Testament*, 4:340–41, s.v. *"luo."*
8. E.g., Mark 13:1–8, 14–20; cf. 4:17; 10:30; Matt. 24:1–8, 15–22; cf. 5:11–12; 10:23; 13:21; Luke 21:5–11, 20–24; cf. 6:22–23; 11:49.
9. Mark 13:9–13; Matt. 24:9–14; Luke 21:12–19.
10. E.g., 1 Kgs. 18:13; 19:14; 2 Chr. 24:20–22; 36:16; Isa. 42:1–9; 49:1–7; 50:4–9a; 52:13–53:12; Jer. 26:20–23; esp. 2 Macc. 2:9–18:36 and 4 Macc. 6:1–18:24.

Chapter 9: The Resurrection

1. E.g., George W. E. Nickelsburg, *Resurrection, Immortality, and Eternal Life in Intertestamental Judaism*, Harvard Theological Studies 26 (Cambridge: Harvard University Press, 1972).
2. For different conceptions, see ibid., 177–80.
3. *2 Bar.* 51:1–3, trans. A. F. J. Klijn in Charlesworth, *Old Testament Pseudepigrapha*, 2:638.
4. On the experience of the living Jesus as the experience of Christian community in antiquity and today, see the eloquent Luke Timothy Johnson, *The Real Jesus: The Misguided Quest for the Historical Jesus and the Truth of the Traditional Gospels* (San Francisco: HarperSanFrancisco, 1996), esp. 141–66.
5. For my answer to the question, What can we believe about eternal life? see Ronald J. Allen, *Wholly Scripture: Preaching Biblical Themes* (St. Louis: Chalice Press, 2004), 1–3, 109–14.

Chapter 10: Jesus in the Gospel of John

1. John does use a little bit of language that has an apocalyptic echo, but apocalypticism does not play a major role in the Fourth Gospel.
2. John uses the term *realm* in the same way that I use the term *sphere* in this chapter: e.g., John 3:3, 5; 18:36.
3. The classic exposition is J. Louis Martyn, *History and Theology in the Fourth Gospel*, 3rd ed., New Testament Library (Louisville, KY: Westminster John Knox Press, 2003).

Chapter 11: Jesus in Gospels outside the Bible

1. I refer to the Protestant version of the Bible with the sixty-six books in the First and Second Testaments. The Roman Catholic Bible contains an additional set of books that are often called the Apocrypha, such as

Wisdom of Solomon, Ecclesiasticus (also known as Sirach or Ben Sira), Tobit, 1 and 2 Maccabees, and other books. The Bible of the Orthodox churches includes all the books found in the Roman Catholic Bible plus even more books. However, none of the Gospels discussed in this chapter are found in Protestant, Roman Catholic, or Orthodox Bibles.

2. For a collection of such materials organized according to literary categories (such as stories relating to the birth and childhood of Jesus, his parents, his ministry, his death and resurrection, Pilate, and Veronica), see J. K. Elliott, *The Apocryphal Jesus: Legends of the Early Church* (New York: Oxford University Press, 1996).

3. On how the church developed the Bible (the canon) as known in Protestant, Roman Catholic, and Orthodox versions today, a concise study is Lee Martin McDonald, *The Formation of the Christian Biblical Canon*, rev. and expanded ed. (Peabody, MA: Hendrickson, 1995).

4. Athanasius, "Festal Letter 39," trans. W. Schneemelcher, in E. Henneke and W. Schneemelcher, eds., *New Testament Apocrypha* (Philadelphia: Westminster Press, 1963), 1:59–60.

5. From "Gospel of the Nazareans," trans. J. K. Elliott, *The Apocryphal New Testament* (New York: Oxford University Press, 1993), 11.

6. From "Gospel of the Ebionites," ibid., 15.

7. Ibid., 14.

8. From "Gospel of Thomas," trans. Thomas O. Lambdin, in James M. Robinson, ed., *The Nag Hammadi Library: The Definitive Translation of the Gnostic Scriptures Complete in One Volume* (San Francisco: HarperSanFrancisco, 1990), 121.

9. *Gospel of Mary*, trans. Karen L. King, from her *The Gospel of Mary of Magdala: Jesus and the First Woman Apostle* (Santa Rosa, CA: Polebridge Press, 2003), 14.

10. Ibid.

11. From "Gospel of Peter," trans. J. K. Elliott, *Apocryphal New Testament*, 154.

12. Ibid., 156–57.

Chapter 12: The Life of Jesus for Today

1. For a fuller explanation of this way of thinking about how to move from the meaning of a text in the past to its meaning for today, see Ronald J. Allen, *Preaching Is Believing: The Sermon as Theological Reflection* (Louisville, KY: Westminster John Knox Press, 2002), 37–62.

2. Clark M. Williamson, *Way of Blessing, Way of Life: A Christian Theology* (St. Louis: Chalice Press, 1998), 81–82.

3. Suetonius, "The Deified Claudius," in *Suetonius*, ed. J. C. Rolfe, Loeb Classical Library (Cambridge: Harvard University Press, 1914), 2:25.4, p. 53.

4. Josephus, *Antiquities,* 18.3.3. (18.63–64); pp. 49–51; 18.5.2 (18.116–19), pp. 81–85; and Josephus, *Jewish Antiquities,* trans. Louis H. Feldman, Loeb Classical Library (Cambridge: Harvard University Press, 1965), 20.9.1, pp. 107–9. Scholars agree that the first passage, 18.3.3, has been edited by Christians to present Jesus in a very favorable light, but many scholars think that the passage originally contained a less elaborate reference to Jesus.

Further Reading

Aland, Kurt, ed. *Synopsis of the Four Gospels.* Rev. ed. New York: United Bible Societies, 1985.

Allen, O. Wesley. *Reading the Synoptic Gospels: Basic Methods for Interpreting Matthew, Mark, and Luke.* St. Louis: Chalice Press, 2000.

Allen, Ronald J., and Clark M. Williamson. *Preaching the Gospels without Blaming the Jews: A Lectionary Commentary.* Louisville, KY: Westminster John Knox Press, 2004.

Dunn, James D. G., and Scott McKnight, eds. *The Historical Jesus in Recent Research.* Winona Lake, IN: Eisenbrauns, 2005.

Powell, Mark Allan. *Jesus as a Figure in History: How Modern Historians View the Man from Galilee.* Louisville, KY: Westminster John Knox Press, 1998.

Sanders, E. P. *The Historical Figure of Jesus.* London: Penguin Books, 1993.

Throckmorton, Burton H., Jr. *Gospel Parallels: A Comparison of the Synoptic Gospels.* 5th ed. Nashville: Thomas Nelson, 1992.